Are You Walking in the Path of Miracles?

GORDON D. VAN NAMEE

© Copyright, 2017

By

Gordon D. Van Namee

ISBN-978-1-5136-2042-8

Library of Congress-in-Publication Data

All rights reserved. No part of this publication may be reproduced, stored in a retrieval system, or transmitted in any form or by any means, electronic, mechanical, photocopying, recording, or otherwise, without the prior written permission of the author and publisher.

Cover designed by Delaney-Designs
Photography

                    REALITY PUBLISHING, INC.
                            5442 Baobab Lane
                          Lake Park, Ga. 31636
                             850-510-7224

Jesus saw Nathanael coming toward Him, and said of Him, "Behold an Israelite indeed, in whom is no deceit!" Nathanael said to Him, "How do You know me?"

Jesus answered and said to him, "Before Philip called you, when you were under the fig tree, I saw you." Nathanael answered and said to Him, "Rabbi, You are the Son of God! You are the King of Israel!" Jesus answered and said to him, "Because I said to you, 'I saw you under the fig tree,' do you believe?

You will see greater things than these." And He said to him,

"Most assuredly, I say to you, hereafter you shall see heaven open, and the angels of God ascending and descending upon the Son of Man."

John 1:47-51

Dedication

This writing is dedicated to the saints of JESUS CHRIST who have remained strong through it all, in the past, and in the present. It is dedicated to those past who have shown us the way as reflected through CHRIST JESUS and to those present who continue to illuminate that reality.

Acknowledgement

This writing could only be accomplished by the work of JESUS through His faithful. That is the story within these pages and the story of life. It is the only lasting reality through it all—the faithful, the strong, and the courageous write the eternal story of life (Joshua 1:9).

I must acknowledge my wife without whose willingness to sacrifice I would not be able to complete this writing. She is a saint that stands strong and I am so thankful that the LORD has blessed me with her.

Much appreciation goes to those who assisted me in bringing this writing to a final conclusion. Those who took the time to proof and give advice were a true gift of Grace. For those who willingly, for the glory of the LORD JESUS CHRIST, allowed me to share their story that this true reality of Grace might be declared, I say—thank you!

Above all, I acknowledge that this writing is given truth and insight through the presence of the HOLY SPIRIT. Through prayer and submission, He played the key role. May all the glory be for JESUS CHRIST, the one Name above all names.

Table of Contents

Introduction 13

    The Reality of Miracles 17

    All Miracles are Radical Acts of JESUS's Love 25

    The Greatest Miracle 29

    Genesis Grace: The Miracle of New Beginnings 37

    Miracles as a Process 45

    The Miracle of the Impossible 55

    The Miracle of the Word 61

    The Miracle of: "In the Name of JESUS!" 69

    The Miracle of Hope 81

    The Miracle of Manna 91

    The Miracle of Healing 97

    Miracles in the Storm 103

    The Miracle of God's Ever Present Invitation 109

    The Miracle of Pure Ecstatic Grace 115

    Living a Miraculous Life 123

    The Miracle of Giving Thanks! 153

    Miracles Abound! 157

Bibliography 161

Join the Miracle 163

Be a Miracle 165

Introduction

"My wife and I are selling all we have and are moving to Guatemala." That is what I heard this morning as I was attending a men's breakfast meeting. The man speaking said, I am leaving my job of thirty-one years, and we are selling our house, vehicles, and all our belongings to go into full-time ministry in one of the poorest countries in the Western Hemisphere. If that weren't enough, he said that they would be located in a village in the western hill country on the other side of a lake, which is only accessible by boat. He told me that shortly after making the decision to take this step into mission work, their daughter told them that she was pregnant with their first grandchild, who would now be born while they were in two different parts of the world. This successful professional and his wife are living the American dream, yet they are willing to give up everything to gain the one thing that is above all—a more complete life in Jesus Christ.

Either this couple is crazy or there is an amazingly great work of God taking place upon their hearts and in their lives. I happen to know this man and can attest to the fact that he is not crazy. He has learned the reality of the presence of God within him and has grown sensitive to the voice of that presence. Yet knowing this and being a man of Christian faith myself, I am still placed into a wondrous awe by the decision of this couple. I am indeed humbled by it. In hearing his story of growth in faith to Jesus Christ through the years and how it has culminated to this greater level of commitment, I realize that it could only happen through the miraculous power of Grace—yes, a Divine action stirring in their lives. Looking from the outside into their situation I see what I can only understand as a living miracle in progress.

A few months ago from this writing I saw the report of a survey, which said that a majority of Christians in the United States no longer believe in miracles. My first thought was, "How sad!" Then my thought turned to the reality that I know—that miracles abound. And I thought how sad it is that Christians are not seeing with spiritual eyes but with darkened worldly eyes; for many, their fire has gone out. This is in stark contrast to the truth and wonder that I heard this morning at that breakfast meeting—two realities, one of a flame of faith burning brightly within the heart, uplifting and encouraging; and one that is sad and wanting, wandering with little to no hope. What this couple symbolizes is the truth that Jesus Christ manifests in the lives of His children through faith.

I don't feel moved to analyze the reasons for why some Christians have lost hope in the reality of God, but I do want to proclaim the truth that other Christians and myself experience on a daily basis—which is that "Miracles through the Lord Jesus Christ abound!" This is simply a fact and Christians need to come back to the power that is in Jesus Christ and be awakened in faith, and they too will see the wonders of Jesus in and about their lives. They may even get close enough to the "fire of the Spirit" to experience the same reality that has been revealed to this couple who are in the midst of moving to Guatemala.

During my thirty-five years of walking with the Lord I have seen and experienced more miracles than I can remember. Miracles are happening each day, often around us; in fact, they abound! If you have any doubts I challenge you to explore this journey. If you believe in miracles then I want you to be encouraged and be delighted in the true stories that are presented in the following pages.

CHAPTER ONE

The Reality of Miracles

That which was from the beginning, which we have heard, which we have seen with our eyes, which we have looked upon, and our hands have handled, concerning the Word of life— the life was manifested, and we have seen, and bear witness, and declare to you that eternal life which was with the Father and was manifested to us—

1 John 1:1-2

Recently, I was visiting a pastor in Kenya, East Africa, and he shared with me some of the most profound stories of the present positive power of Jesus Christ in his ministry. Yet, before I heard him share these stories, I realized there was an immediate miracle involving this pastor—that his very life was a living miracle. He serves a church in Eldoret, Kenya called the Bread of Life Church. It is a humble church structure by Western standards with sheet metal sides and roof, no insulation or inner wall; just sheet metal attached to exposed roughly cut boards. The floor is concrete, which, for many churches in Kenya, is a significant upgrade. There is no interior ceiling; just open space stands above the rows of cheap plastic chairs. The road leading up to the church is dirt and rough with deep ravines sure to quickly deplete a car's shock absorbers.

Upon my first visit there as I entered the church campus, I felt awash in the power of Christ's love in that place. It was as if an enormous wave of Christ's love had splashed over me—it was real and palpable—I experienced it! The first thing that came to mind are the words from John 3:16: "For God so loved the world that He gave His only begotten Son, that whoever believes in Him should not perish but have everlasting life." Those two words, "so loved," jumped out at me in the depth of my mind. I could actually feel the overwhelming love of Christ in that church.

Surrounding this austere church is a horseshoe structure of buildings, built in the same fashion, housing classrooms for about 150 children. These children are from very poor families that could not otherwise afford to go to school. Some are orphans caused by the AIDS epidemic and some are children of single mothers who can hardly exist on their wages and do not have the funds to pay for public schools.

The church family comes from the poorest of the city. I can assure you that their weekly offering does not even come close to one hundred American dollars. It most likely would be in the range of thirty to forty dollars. One of the ways they support this ministry is by housing rabbits, from which they collect the waste and then sell the fertilizer to farmers. Can you imagine how long it takes to fill a fifty-gallon drum with rabbit waste? Who would go to this length, to this degree?

So what I experienced was the miracle of the power of Jesus Christ's love alive in the pastor and his wife and that church family. Against all possibilities they are caring for the least and the last in society. They are not doing it to better their material status or to build a power structure in this world, but to exercise their belief in the power of Jesus Christ in the reality of those two words, "so loved." This church family has become the "so loved" of God in that place—as Jesus walked so they walk.

The pastor, his wife, and church family stand against the uncaring social structure to touch the children and their family members with the living love of Jesus Christ. They live a life of sacrifice for the glory of the present reality of Jesus. I was humbled and uplifted at the same time. In that church I saw the reality of God's love in pure Gospel power being lived out.

This picture was taken at the entrance of the Bread of Life Church and COMIDO School. This is a typical Kenyan street. The walls and gate around the church speak to the reality of the violence in their society. Yet, against these conditions, they stand strong.

Here Pastor Simani is with his family posing in front of a classroom building.

This invites us to think about what a miracle is. We often want to see lightning and hear thunder and see mountains split asunder, but as we are told in Scripture in 1 Kings 19:11-12, God often comes in a "still small voice." In this book I want to challenge you to rethink what the dynamics of a miracle are and how miracles manifest—some are lightning and thunder, some are soft and gentle in nature. Some miracles are disruptive and situation-changing; some are subtle and edifying or encouraging. Miracles can be seen in and throughout the life of the faithful if the faithful allow themselves to see through the "eyes of Jesus." To see through the eyes of Jesus one must first accept that they live in Jesus's reality. Apostle Paul declares in Acts 17:28, "For in Him we live and move and have our being."

The other night traveling on the interstate I saw a sunset that I would put into the classification of a miracle. It was so brilliant in its spectrum of light and shades of color that it glowed. The colors were as only God could paint. I paused and said a prayer of praise and thanksgiving for experiencing such a sight of His presence.

That is a key phase, "experiencing His presence." Ultimately that is what a miracle is. **It is the Divine positive movement of Jesus Christ in and upon the lives of His children for their salvation, growth, and edification of relationship and welfare, which takes place in and throughout creation in order to enhance the reality of His kingdom present.** Within this encompassing definition there are many aspects. All of these aspects center upon the active engaging presence of Jesus Christ in the lives of His children. It is in this engaging presence that Jesus hopes for the salvation and fulfillment of the created order of His children (Jeremiah 29:11).

When Moses lifted up his hand at the crossing of the Red Sea he could do nothing without the engaging presence of the Lord. Exodus 14:21 states: "Then Moses stretched out his hand over the sea; and the Lord caused the sea to go back by a strong east wind all that night, and made the sea into dry land, and the waters were divided." When the Lord directly engages in our lives miracles occur, and if our senses are alert we will see His movement in and though us and about us in some form. This is the perspective that we are given in 14:19 when we are told, "And the Angel of God, who went before the camp of Israel, moved and went behind them and the pillar of cloud went from before them and stood behind them." They were engulfed in the presence of the Lord.

King David was very sensitive to the presence of the Lord. In Psalm 16 and repeated in Act 2:25-26, he proclaims, "I foresaw the Lord always before my face, for He is at my right hand, that I may not be shaken. Therefore my heart rejoiced, and my tongue was glad." A living and present relationship is what David was expressing. Yet, this living and present relationship could have been foul and ugly, but for the reality that the Lord Jesus Christ is love, kindness, and compassion (1John 4:7- 8; Mark 6:34). David realized the presence of the Lord in the midst of the problems of the world and he knew these problems well: a son who turned against him and who was ultimately killed, as well as the death of a young child. Yet, David stood in the realized presence of Jesus in that place and said, "I foresaw the Lord always before my face." Isn't that a miracle; that when we walk through the "valley of the shadow of death,"—which is our life's journey in this place—that we can have a state of "blessed assurance"? Isn't it a miracle that in the darkest of moments we can sense the light of hope in our hearts and understand that the Lord will work everything out even when it often times looks impossible?

In Psalm 121, David cries out in the first verse, "I will lift up my eyes to the hills—from whence comes my help?" He is acknowledging that in the midst of life's struggles our strength is not enough; we need the presence of a greater power. Then in verse two, as a statement of reflection, he proclaims, "My help comes from the Lord, who made heaven and earth." What is happening between those two verses? There seems to be a void between the two. The first is a statement of despair and the second is a statement of known supernatural assistance upon his life. What happened between these two verses is a gulf of realized presence of the Lord in his life—a life filled with miracles in which faith becomes a reality.

Looking at David's life we can see that he has been in many situations where his strength was not sufficient, but he has so often seen the Lord engage and assist him that his faith became certainty—no longer looking into the uncertain but into the realized face of Jesus. By faith, he had built such a strong relationship with the Lord that there was no question as to the presence of the Lord being with him. In that way, faith grows in maturity to be a certainty, and thus the phrase, "I know that I know that I know!" That mature certainty of faith that David expresses and lives out is **a miracle of realized relationship with the Divine.**

What I am stressing to you is that miracles abound when we let our spiritual senses open up to the reality of the Lord's presence with us. Miracles take many forms and affect us each day in many ways. For Christians the greatest miracle is life itself, because life is being able to experience and take joy in the living relationship of a perfect loving God as known in the living reality of Jesus Christ. **In this way, salvation is both an incipient miracle and the greatest miracle for it opens the door to a life of miraculous living**. Without salvation we would be left deaf and blind to the living and engaging presence of Jesus Christ.

Opening our spiritual eyes to this new understanding of miracles allows us to say with King David, "I foresaw the Lord always before my face" and I know that "He is at my right hand, that I may not be shaken" and "my heart rejoiced, and my tongue was glad" (Psalm 16; Act 2:25-26). **In the kingdom reality of Jesus Christ, in this place, miracles and the experiencing of God are one**. This is true for those who have the spiritual sensitivity to see in the realm of Jesus's Grace and understand it by the power of the Holy Spirit who lives within them and provides Divine teachings and clarity. In this way, the Christian is called to live in a new reality and to grow into this new reality to a mature state—it takes time and focus.

Living in the known reality of miracles does not mean that the mountains have to split before our eyes, though that might be the case. It can also mean that the soft and subtle love of Jesus Christ is moving upon and though His saints, the faithful, to reshape the wrong into right, the dark into light, and the hurt and pain into joy! I have seen a range of miracles before my eyes; some I sense instantly and others I have to process and reflect upon. But with each miracle, I understand it to be **the experience of the living presence of Jesus Christ. He was raised from the dead and is now alive and engaged in the life of His children, even today**. It is His heart to bless His children that they might see with eyes that go beyond the lowly worldly realm.

If we, as the faithful of Jesus Christ, do not have the spiritual sensitivity to see His work around us then we will miss the wonder and beauty that He so wants us to know. **The reality is that miracles abound around us all the time and we must recalibrate our spiritual eyes and ears to discern them and give thanks and praise in the sensing of this truth.** It is with this understanding that I invite you to come on this journey. It may be new to you or it may be an edification or encouragement, but wherever you are in your faith-walk, I do believe that we all can be changed through the power of His love into a deeper walk with Him.

CHAPTER TWO

All Miracles are Radical Acts of JESUS's Love

For God so loved the world that He gave his only begotten Son, that whoever believes in Him should not perish but have everlasting life.

John 3:16

The word radical means rooted in the source. *Webster's* defines it as, "Arising from or reaching a root or source: basic; drastic, extreme." As the love of Jesus is pure and holy and He is full of "grace and truth" (John 1:14), we can see how He sharply contrasts against the way of this world, which is deceptive, exclusive, closed, and often hurtful. Jesus is the very essence of pure Love, Truth, and Grace. He is the source through which all must be realized and measured.

So whether one sees the miracle of God speaking softly through His children as exemplified by the pastor and his wife in Kenya, or one sees the lightning and thunder of God's movement in a more drastic way, it is all radical. All miracles emanate out of the purity of perfect Love, Truth, and Grace, and they all are equally great and wondrous; however, some have a more profound effect upon creation than others. When we view our lives through a theological lens or as is better said, "through the eyes of Jesus," we can see value in the presence of JESUS with us at any level of movement.

Pastor Simani, whom you met in the first chapter, shared with me the following story of the radical love of Jesus. Twelve years ago, he was called to go and see his sister who was dying from AIDS. She was tested HIV positive and through the course of time got weaker and weaker. As she was nearing death, the family carried her and placed her in the living room of their home for visitors to come and say their goodbyes. It is common in that part of the world for the neighbors to stay until the last breath to offer comfort in passing. Pastor Simani and others continued to pray for her and miraculously, she was healed. It has been twelve years since her healing and she is still doing well.

In Kenya, tens of thousands of people have died from AIDS. For Pastor Simani's sister, the medical help was not what it is today. Even today, Kenya is not that medically advanced. However, God heard the prayers and responded in a radical way—in a way of mercy and grace. It was a Divine act of "engaging Holy Love." There were no doctors nor was there medicine, only prayers to the one true God who delights in being engaged in our lives. Our part of this "Holy Equation" is faith—that is all and everything—"The just shall live by faith" (Romans 1:17). On the one side of the equation is a perfect loving God willing to bless His children, and this God has "Absolute Power" to accomplish whatever He pleases. On the other side of the equation is the need for the created to respond to the initiatives of the Creator. The response required is that of an intimate loving relationship from a genuine and earnest heart, through prayer, initiated by faith. The heart is the fertile ground of the realized relationship and the prayer is the active participation in that relationship. Another way of saying this is that **prayer is the active participation in the reality of GOD.** Thus the act of prayer, with an earnest and wanting heart, becomes an act of participation in the greatest living miracle—being joined into the living presence of Jesus Christ. This particular healing was aside from doctors or medicine, but let me be clear—doctors and medicine are blessings of Grace. They are often used as instruments in the process of miracles. The question then becomes, once the instrument is used to facilitate the miracle, do we become blind to the wonder of Jesus's hand that orchestrates such a miracle?

One cannot explain why the pastor's sister was healed and others are not. I have prayed for many people who were not healed in this realm, and I have prayed for many people who were healed. It is God's choice and reasoning. **All of His work is good**. The difficulty for humans is that we often only see through worldly vision and not spiritual vision. **Spiritual vision is far greater, and by its nature, more radical than worldly vision.** One thing we must keep in mind is that the greatest healing is to go and be with the Lord in that place of "perfect eternal life." If we could understand the wonder and the joy of living in His presence and the perfect peace in that place then we may understand the joy of not being healed in this lower physical realm.

Miracles are not about mysteries and ghosts. Yes, there is a degree of mystery but miracles are a continuation of the reality of Jesus Christ being engaged with the life of humanity. As He walked this earth Jesus preformed many healings and miracles during His three years of recorded ministry. **The context has changed but the reality is the same—Jesus Christ is God with us, who is pouring out His Love and Grace upon us to this day.**

All of His love and acts are radical, life-changing, and life-forming. Jesus is the Creator and sustainer of all life, the "WORD" made flesh that we can see the reality of the Father's love towards us. He delights in us when His children are experiencing and responding to His love and engaged presence.

To join into the reality of this life of living wonder you must simply say, "Yes!" to Jesus and invite Him into your heart. Then you must be wholly intentional about this new relationship and hold it as the most precious treasure within you. "But we have this treasure in earthen vessels, that the excellence of the power may be of God and not of us" (2 Corinthians 4:7). This most precious treasure must be protected, cherished, delighted in, and held ever so close to your heart. It is the most precious gift that you can have in all of creation. It is appropriate to respond to such a gift with praise and thanksgiving and to remember that the power is not ours but a wondrous gift from the Father through Jesus Christ.

CHAPTER THREE

The Greatest Miracle

For all the promises of God in Him are Yes, and in Him Amen, to the glory of God through us. Now He who establishes us with you in Christ and has anointed us is God, who also has sealed us and given us the Spirit in our hearts as a guarantee.

2 Corinthians 1:20-22

When God broke into creation with the birth of His Son Jesus Christ the normalcy of creation was shattered! A new creation was being formed—yes, a new Genesis was taking place and it was in the process of revealing itself in its fullness. The WORD, who is Christ Jesus, was made flesh. Here He was not just speaking creation into being as before, but was now joining into creation and calling this new creation to be one with His being. God, no longer a bystander, stepped into creation in the likeness of Jesus Christ to walk with His children and gave them the liberty to walk in His reality. Because of this, the angel said to them, "Do not be afraid for behold, I bring you good tidings of great joy which will be to all people. For there is born to you this day in the city of David a Savior, who is Christ the Lord" (Luke 2:10-11). And there was "a multitude of the heavenly host praising

God and saying: "Glory to God in the highest, and on earth peace, goodwill toward men!" (Luke 2:10-14).

The birth of Jesus was a "Hallelujah" moment! A new creation was formed and that new creation is the present kingdom of the living reality of Jesus Christ. God, through His Son Jesus Christ, invites His children not only to return to Him (John 1:12), but also to be born of Him (John 1:13). The birth of Jesus was the breaking-in of the kingdom of God into a dead creation in order to bring new life, new awareness into the senses of His created children—to "as many as received Him" (John 1:12). The kingdom of God is entered into and realized through Jesus Christ, and His birth into creation is a "Hallelujah" invitation to this eternal reality.

There is no greater miracle than this in all of created existence. Not just that we are created, but that we as His created have the ability to come alive in Him. That our senses would no longer be dulled, our ears no longer blocked, our eyes no longer blinded—but that shattering of darkness as He entered into creation is the same shattering that will break into our hearts and minds and start a new Genesis creation within each of us—if we will but wholly open up our hearts and bring Him in.

This is the living miracle that continues to spark the light of creation in the hearts of God's children. Each time a child is saved and born anew into Christ Jesus it is a "Hallelujah" event! **This Genesis act is a creation act of new potential for a life of miraculous living!** Ponder upon that for a moment. If you have accepted Jesus into your heart and are a believing Christian, that is not just a miracle of an event, but of a life that is meant to be miraculous. Are you taking advantage of this offering that Jesus freely gives you?

As I write, this comes to mind: I was serving a church as their pastor and it was a loving and Spirit-filled church. One Sunday, one of our younger members, a young adult, brought with her a friend who was visiting from out of town. Her friend was wearing all black clothes and her hair had been cut as short as possible. If I recall correctly, she was even wearing black lipstick. She had facial piercings and an expression of gloom set upon her face. I remember approaching her to greet her, with some degree of trepidation, and she refused to acknowledge me. My response was, "We sure are glad that you are with us today!" Amazingly, the next Sunday she was back. That pleasantly confounded me. I thought, "How is God working in this situation? Lord, this is a tough one!"

Many members of the church family greeted and loved upon her. Over the next few weeks I saw a dramatic transformation. She set aside her black attire and started to wear bright-colored clothes, and she was also letting her hair grow long. This was not in a day or two; it proceeded over a period of several months. No longer was her face a face of gloom, but it now reflected joy and happiness. Then came the Sunday that really surprised me, as the choir came down the center aisle to open our service, there she was with them, singing joyfully! As I share this with you, I can feel the tears running down my face. I was so joyful for her and the remembrance of it still moves my heart. She had been set free and was enfolded in the community of God's love. His arms reached out around her and she felt the love and responded to Jesus with an eternal "Yes!"

That was a Genesis movement of Jesus Christ upon the life of one of His children. He broke into her heart and took birth in that place and started to grow and mature within her. It was life-changing, life-forming, and life-growing. It was a living miracle that we all watched. It was radical in the sense that the love of Jesus Christ, the one true source of perfect love, was poured into her by the Holy Spirit (Romans 5:5). I still, to this day, remember the joy I felt as I was honored to minister the baptism—the consummation of this new birth, this miracle.

The greatest miracle is the miracle of salvation, without which no miracle would be understood to any meaningful degree. If you have received Jesus into your heart you are a living miracle! It is a miracle grounded in His work, His movement in your life, by the power of His grace: "For by grace you have been saved through faith, and that not of yourselves; it is the gift of God" (Ephesians 2:8).

In the same church, I witnessed many Christians returning to the Lord after many years, people in their fifties and sixties, which during that time, was the vast majority of the congregation. It is not uncommon, though certainly unfortunate, for a person to receive Christ and then return to the way of the world or get caught up in the busyness of life and forget about Jesus. This can happen to all of us. Even to pastors. We must remember that treasure within and how precious it is. It must be protected at all costs. Without Jesus we are nothing more than tumbleweeds blowing across the desert of life.

Again and again I saw the miracle of Jesus working in the hearts of His children to call them home, to reignite that fire within. They were from all walks of life—teachers, chemists, and administrators—all seeking more in life. For many of these people, returning to the faith in an active way was the evidence of their discovery that Jesus was not just a nice thought or a set of ideas, but a living and active intimate relationship that can be experienced. They wanted to go to the source of truth where they could be real in themselves and find the one real God within.

One of the most moving movements in that ministry was when a member of the church family asked me to go and visit his sister at the hospital who was close to passing. He told me that she didn't believe in Jesus. He warned me that I may not be well received, but he asked me to go and I did.

I walked into her room where I saw her laying in the hospital bed. I greeted her. A friend was with her but soon left and there we were, just the two of us. I told her that I had come there to tell her how much Jesus loved her. She responded by telling me that she didn't think that Jesus cared anything about her. Then she opened up to me and shared her deep hurt and pains. I explained to her that Jesus felt those pains and has always wanted to comfort her. I wanted her to see that Jesus does not cause the pain and suffering that exists in this broken world; that is **NOT** His will for us. He wants good for us. I spoke to her of His tender love for her and how He esteems her and then I shared the reality of eternity—its substance of perfect life and joy for evermore. At one point in my journey with Jesus He opened the portals of Heaven and let me taste the reality of life in Heaven, so it was from that source (yes, a radical thought) that I shared with her. I could see wondrous peace come over her and in that place she accepted Jesus back into her heart and I anointed her with the water of our tears. It was her re-baptism and a most holy moment that was created by the movement of the present Holy Spirit of God. No one on Earth could have pre-scripted this or engineered it so instantaneously—but only by Divine engagement! It was a Holy moment that I will cherish until I go and am with the Lord in that final place.

There are many reasons we go astray. There is only one source that can give us wholeness and blessed comfort, and only one source that can bring us back to Him—the power of His present love. She passed three days after our visit and did so with Jesus in her heart. He was waiting for her with arms open wide to receive her into His living Grace. That was a miracle of intervention by Jesus who gave it another try—you see, He **NEVER** gives up!

Jesus calls one Word and only one Word into creation and that is the "Yes!" of His being. It is the "Yes!" of His eternal promise. It took a miracle of His Grace to be with me that day that I could speak His words into this closed heart. That day, as I walked from my car to her hospital room, I prayed constantly—"Lord, help me to be a useful vessel for You." Not by my strength or wisdom but by the Grace of Jesus Christ through His Holy Spirit, I was given the words that needed to be spoken.

As I look back at it, it was a series of miracles caught up in the greater reality of a living miracle known as Grace. **Grace is the realm of existence within the presence of Jesus Christ.** As Christians we are born into Christ. Galatians 2:20 says, "I have been crucified with Christ; it is no longer I who live, but Christ lives in me; and the life which I now live in the flesh I live by faith in the Son of God, who loved me and gave Himself for me." John 14:20 says, "At that day you will know that I am in My Father, and you in Me, and I in you." So we are born into Christ and He is alive in us. We are one together. This is the greatest of miracles—the living supernatural physics of a living miracle—"For all the promises of God in Him are Yes, and in Him Amen, to the glory of God through us" (2 Corinthians 1:20).

The miracle of salvation is not complete without the Cross of Jesus, the Resurrection, and Pentecost—all stages of new birth and new formation. Salvation is a progression of growth. It is both instant and lifelong. The realm of the Divine—the path of the miraculous—touches each part of the journey.

The birth of Jesus calls forth what follows. His purpose is to bring each of us to completion (Philippians 1:6). His assisting hand of Grace is there to help us and to enable us to move towards Him. Jesus's Cross clears the way, His resurrection shows us the truth and points to His reality, and Pentecost invites us to join Him, offering us the empowerment for the journey. Miracle upon miracle—that's miraculous living!

Jesus tells us in John 15:11, "These things I have spoken to you, that My joy may remain in you, and that your joy may be full." Joy and the presence of the Divine go together. **The reality of the miracle is realizing the joy of His presence with us.** So, I have another question for you—can the world really give you true joy? Do you want true joy? Jesus wants you to have true joy. That is why He came to Earth, hung on a cross, arose and ascended to Heaven, and sent the Holy Spirit down to dwell within the faithful. The fruit of a life with Jesus is love, peace, joy, faithfulness, self-control, patience, gentleness, kindness, and generosity. The decision has always been yours. He says, "Yes!" and He waits for your answer.

CHAPTER FOUR

Genesis Grace: The Miracle of New Beginnings

Therefore, if anyone is in Christ, he or she is a new creation; old things have passed away; behold, all things have become new.

2 Corinthians 5:17

Each day is a miracle of Genesis proportions. Each day we awake to new possibilities and new potential. That is if we have positioned ourselves properly with the Lord and accepted the potential of such a relationship. Each day we start a new life in Him. It is in this understanding that we hope anew and afresh each day. It is in this vein that we strive to do His will and accomplish it in His righteousness. If obstacles, failings, and worldly pressures beset us, we can take renewed strength in this movement of Divine Love that will never give up on us, but will move upon us and in us with a force of Genesis Grace. We often live in a state of self-condemnation and guilt but the Lord lives in a state of Genesis expectation of us. He places His concern not on our failures of yesterday or a minute ago but upon the very presence of "now" and tomorrow. The reality of the "now" of our lives will create tomorrow. Seeking His will brings the faithful into harmony with this Genesis force.

The Genesis force requires that the faithful make the shift into a kingdom reality and receive the awareness that Jesus's authority is real and supreme. It requires the faithful to be immersed wholly into Jesus—heart, mind, and soul. It also requires daily spiritual connecting through prayer, Scripture, and fasting. As believers, we should join often in community fellowship with other believers. This will help to keep our relationship with the Lord vibrant and alive.

In doing this, our perspective of each day will change. Imagine awakening each morning to the feeling of a complete and fresh start. That should be the reality of any Christian. We should not carry the burdens of one day into the other nor should we anticipate the burdens of the next day to come. As Paul so clearly tells us in Philippians 4, "Be anxious for nothing." As believers, ours is to be present in each moment of the day—to live each day fully and make the most of it. This is placing our faith upon Jesus and not oneself. You can still make plans for the future, but live each day in the fullness of His righteousness, so that you may be at peace knowing you have given Him all that you have. It means at the end of each day as we settle into rest, we give Him prayerful thanksgiving for that day and take peace in His Grace to protect us for the challenges and opportunities of the next day.

Think of the burden this would remove from you. Think how much better you would feel without the stress of the world upon you each night and each morning as you face another day. What I am asking you to do is face a "new" day as a "new" creation with "new" creational possibilities. Live in the full potential of Jesus Christ!

Throughout the day and especially each night I say the Lord's Prayer and this cleanses me of all the "what ifs" of that day. It cleanses me of any potential guilt or resentments in my spirit and sets the groundwork for the next creation awakening. If we earnestly strive to do the will of Jesus and remain humble before Him with a repentant heart then we can awaken knowing that **Jesus has forgiven all of our shortcomings and wishes us into this new day with the fullness of His Grace and the Holy Spirit within us to guide us.**

So as the sun rises each day to re-anoint the earth with the blessing of light that will bring forth new growth in creation, so the Lord shines upon our hearts and souls each day with new possibilities. Jesus is a Genesis God bringing forth new beginnings and second chances. I saw this miraculous Genesis Grace lived out in the life of a Christian brother. As he told me his life story I could see the movement of Jesus's Divine Love threaded throughout his life. **This movement of Divine Love is the creating power of new life and it is repeated throughout the Bible stories and throughout our lives as a force of Genesis Grace.**

I met Charles a little over a year ago. It was at a Kairos gathering. Kairos is a worldwide Christian organization that does prison ministry. This meeting happened at a prison in Southern Georgia. As a group of faithful Christians, we go into Valdosta State Prison every Monday night for a gathering with the inside Kairos members. It often takes different forms. Sometimes we have speakers and sometimes the men gather into prayer and share groups. Twice a year, once in the spring and once in the fall, we offer a three and one-half day intensive Kairos weekend for the inmates (who we refer to as residents). These are convicted felons. Some will be out in a few years and some will never get out. During the weekend the residents have the opportunity to direct their lives towards a new path—it's their choice, we just make the offering.

Charles's prison journey first began in the state of Florida. It started when he was seventeen years old. He was brought up in the church but became rebellious and in his words he refused to listen to the loving advice of his grandmother and other relatives. He decided to move out and went on his own. On his eighteenth birthday he was sentenced to prison. The length of the sentence was between six months and up to five years depending upon his behavior. That was the start of a series of imprisonments that consumed most of his life up unto the age of forty-seven. He said when he got out of prison for any length of time he would do alcohol and weed and soon find himself back in prison.

When I asked him if he had a relationship with God at the time of his prison encounters he told me that he did, but it wasn't the way God wanted it. He said that he "used God and played with God but was never sincere about a real relationship with God." His total motivation at the time was directed towards his own self-pleasure, whatever that was at any given moment. The first time he entered prison was in June of 1979, and it wasn't until 2008, that things started to change. That was twenty-nine years of his life spent in meaninglessness—a life with no certain direction. He wasn't aware of it at the time but the God that he was making fun of never gave up on him and continued to reach out to him in the hope that he would say a truthful, "Yes!"

During one of Charles's periods of incarceration his cousin was sent to the same prison with a twenty-year sentence. The two of them had contact within the prison system. His cousin had been on a Kairos weekend and had given his life over to Jesus Christ in an earnest effort to change his life's direction. He encouraged Charles to do the same, telling him, "You need to change." He obviously saw what Charles could not see—the meaningless downward-spinning cycle that was Charles's life. But Charles just didn't take God seriously and refused to have any part of it. **God will never force a person to say yes to Him but He will place them in positions where they have to face the reality of His Truth and Love.** That is what he did with Charles.

His cousin sent an application to the prison Chaplain on Charles's behalf to attend a Kairos weekend. Charles was not happy about this and he refused to go. But if he didn't go he would be placed in the 'hole'— solitary confinement. He said he didn't like either choice but took the weekend at Kairos just to get out of being sent to the hole. The Kairos weekend started on a Thursday night with introductions, a simple meal, and instructions for the next few days. He said he hated it, and couldn't find anything good about the weekend. On the third day, Saturday, he said they received some letters written to them from school children. He read one letter from a young girl who explained that her father was in prison and that she had missed out on knowing what it was like to have a father. She said, "My dad is in prison and I am growing up without a father—and I'm telling you what I would tell my father: we need our fathers to show us the things and ways of life—please get out and stay out!" He said it was this letter that reached into his heart and touched him in a way that nothing else could have. He said, "It moved more than my heart, it opened my eyes." He asked himself the question, "Do I want to continue or change?" It was at that moment he decided to make a change in his life and asked God in the earnestness of his heart to give him a second chance.

He said that God spoke to him and said, "I never gave up on you." And then God said, "There are always going to be tests in life but you have to overcome them. My Son shed His blood for your sin!" This conversation with God and the words that God spoke framed a new reality for Charles and gave him the hope and courage that he needed to make this radical change. It was on December 21, 2009, that Charles was released from prison—thirty years from the date of that initial sentence.

That is how I met Charles. He is now gainfully employed, and has now joined the Kairos team that ministers to the inmates. He tells his story in the hope that others will listen and hear the message that can change their lives as his was changed. And this is his message: there is always hope from a real and engaging God in the form of Jesus Christ, who will never give up on you and who uses His power to change all things for the better.

This movement of God's Grace in a Genesis mode is part of the pattern of the salvation process. It is not just for the process of justification but it also works in and through the sanctification process to bring His faithful to a higher and deeper place of His love and reality. This process is beautifully called out by Jesus in His conversation with Peter in John 21:15-19. At the point of this conversation Peter has already had many movements in his life of Genesis Grace. Yet, here Jesus is very clear about the purpose and that is to move Peter to a higher and deeper place in His love. Jesus says to Peter three times, "Simon, son of Jonah, do you love Me?" What follows is a progression in the advancement of maturity of faith. First, "Feed My lambs," then, "Tend My sheep" and finally, "Feed My sheep." Each time the emphasis is on the commitment to depend upon and love Jesus more completely. Jesus closes the conversation by saying, "Most assuredly, I say to you, when you were younger, you girded yourself and walked where you wished; but when you are old, you will stretch out your hands, and another will gird you and carry you where you do not wish." **The progression is from novice to fulfillment—a progression of faith to maturity.** As Jesus uses this final thought to signify "by what death" Peter would glory God, He also proclaims another Genesis movement of Grace upon the life of Peter. Through each stage of the conversation, the three "do you love Me" statements and the final statement of glorifying God, denotes a new beginning: an advancement to a higher level.

Genesis Grace is not only a factor in the initial salvation movement and in justification, but is also an aspect of the larger process known as Sanctifying Grace. Whether it happens in one moment or in a series of events, it is all for the purpose of bringing each of us to a fuller meaning of life. For Charles it was a series of miracles: the miracle of a cousin being used as the vessel of God; the miracle of a young girl pouring out her heart to someone she had never met before; the miracle of the spoken word of God into his heart; and that ultimate movement of his heart being led by the Grace of the living presence of Jesus Christ. All of this happened by the power of Jesus who will NEVER give up on Charles or you or me!

Charles has started a new journey of life and now sees through a different lens of reality. He knows that miracles are not only possible but that they are a means through which the Lord exercises His love towards us, His children, that we might come and share His joy in this place. This happened because of the reality of miracles in the here and now of eternal life.

CHAPTER FIVE

Miracles as a Process

Sanctify yourselves, for tomorrow the LORD will do wonders among you.

Joshua 3:5

Some miracles happen over time; not all are instant. In fact, if we look at God's desire to bring His Chosen people into the Promised Land and out of bondage, it took forty years for the fulfillment of His desire. God is more concerned with the character development of His children and their willingness to walk in righteousness than He is in a worldly pre-set time limit for completion of a miracle. Since God honors our decisions as a matter of our "grace freed will," he also responds to the ever-changing dynamics of those decisions. I believe each of us can sense this in our own lives as we reflect on the "what ifs" of life—such is the case with Moses and the people of Israel who journeyed to the Promised Land. The journey of the Israelites out of bondage and into the Promised Land is a series of miracles within a larger miracle. Consider the scene at the Burning Bush, the process of convincing Moses to go before Pharaoh, the Nine Plagues, the death of the firstborn, the water flowing out of the rock of Horeb, and the Manna from Heaven that appeared on the ground each day without which they would not have been sustained. These and more individual miracles happened within the larger context of being brought out of bondage and into the Land of Promise.

Some might say, "That is the Bible and its stories are so far out." However, I tell you that these miracles are happening each day throughout creation. Let me share with you one such miracle that I experienced through a different pastor friend who lives in Kenya, Africa. This living miracle didn't last forty years, but instead, took place sixteen years ago and is still ongoing. And like the journey of Moses to the Promised Land, there were individual miracles within the larger context. But what I want to convey to you by way of this particular miracle is that sometimes, miracles are not instantaneous, but rather, a process over time.

Sixteen years ago I was attending a weekend seminar at Beeson Divinity School in Birmingham, Alabama. I arrived at the appropriate time in the morning. It was a pleasant morning; the sun was shining and it was reasonably warm. It was a beautiful campus and I was in a spirit of great expectation of what the Lord would do that day. I approached the building that I was directed to for registration. Outside of the building there was a courtyard where people were gathering. I walked up to the gathering point to find my way to registration. I stood there for a few moments to get my bearings and I noticed a man standing alone by himself. He was a black man and for some reason he didn't appear to me to be an American. I approached him and greeted him. I asked him where he was from and he told me Kenya, Africa. I asked him what brought him all the way to America and he told me, "I have come to share my story." Without processing the thought, it just came out of my mouth, and I said, "Why don't you come to Florida?" He responded, "All right I will."

We did not know each other and yet we both had made a commitment to travel together and to start a faith-journey together. I was a little shocked at myself and that morning during the classes I was questioning the sanity of my impulsive offering. I made the decision that during the lunch break I would try to get a grip over the situation. I saw my new friend standing alone and approached him and again before I could process any thoughts I said, "Are you coming to Florida?"

And he immediately said, "Yes, I am coming to Florida." Later I learned that he had been handing out his business cards to various people only to find these same cards discarded, lying on tables and chairs. He said he prayed and the Lord told him that he would bring the one he wanted him to meet—I knew nothing of this at the time. Like with Moses, this grace empowered meeting was a miracle in the process of forming a larger miracle.

So there I was traveling five hours south into Florida with a man from Africa that I had never before met. The night before I called my wife and told her what I was doing—certainly she thought I was out of my mind. The faith reality is that when we walk in the power of the Holy Spirit, as we are told in Galatians 5:25, we must take risks. These risks must be linked to a process of discernment and the testing of the spirit.

This brings out an important feature of miracles. **We are often called to be participants in the miracle process.** Miracles are not just "zap actions" taken upon our lives. Miracles have different properties for different circumstances—in other words, one size does not necessarily fit all situations. This was true of Mary's invitation in the birth of Jesus. Her response was to accept being involved in the miracle process. This was also true for her cousin Elizabeth in the birth of John the Baptist.

It wasn't too long into the situation when I knew the Holy Spirit was directing this meeting of the two of us. Our meeting was not a coincidence or an accident. **There is no such thing as a random act in the kingdom of God.** All actions in the kingdom of God are Grace empowered and within the sovereign authority of Jesus Christ. There are willful choices but no random actions. Jesus tells us in Matthew 28:18, "All authority has been given to Me in heaven and on earth." Christians give themselves up to the authority of Jesus Christ but not to the understanding of chaos—which is what random dictates (without authority or directed purpose). Romans 6:14 tell us, "For sin shall not have dominion over you, for you are not under law but under grace." Nor are we, as Christians, under the sway of the world—but under Grace, for "He who dwells in the secret place of the Most High shall abide under the shadow of the Almighty. I will say of the Lord, 'He is my refuge and my fortress'" (Psalm 91).

I arrived home with this new friend and he stayed with us for five weeks. During that time we visited many churches in the northern Florida area. The churches that I served received him with Christian love. I am sure at some point they must have wondered why he was staying so long, but I had accepted it as the will of God. My wife, being the saint that she is, even though she was uncomfortable with the length of the stay, accepted it—another miracle of grace.

The story my new friend wanted to tell was his faith story. He wanted people to know what was happening in

East Africa with the AIDS crisis. How the children were being left to live on the streets with no safety network to protect them. He shared his heart that he wanted to provide for them and bring the much-needed teachings of Jesus to God's children and to enable them to live prosperous lives. He shared how poor the people of Kenya were and asked for help in his ministry. He raised over $20,000 in those five weeks and it was of great benefit to the ministry in Kenya. That $20,000 was another miracle. Yes, there were some struggles in this five-week process and some disappointments, but God is always faithful and what was needed was provided (1 Corinthians 1:9).

During the next two years we stayed in touch and I made a trip to visit him in Eldoret, Kenya. I found a very poor country by Western standards. The reality of the street children broke my heart. The unemployment rate was over fifty percent and the people in the distant villages were truly dirt poor. Yet, in all of this they had a joyful spirit as a people, at least the many that I encountered.

The process of miracles in the pastor's life was about to continue. He told me of a vision that he had been given from the Lord. He said he was walking across a piece of land overlooking the city of Eldoret where he and his wife lived and the Lord spoke to his heart and told him that he was to build a church on that land. He didn't have any money, he didn't own the land, and he didn't even know who owned it, yet that was the directive. He took me to show me the property and as we walked on the land he stopped and asked me to pray for it to become a reality. I must confess that I thought this was so far out of the realm of possibilities that I struggled to offer an earnest prayer.

I gathered what spiritual strength was within me, girded up my spiritual loins, and proceeded to pray. My faith level was admittedly low because I was—for a moment—looking through worldly eyes and not the eyes of the present and infinite power of Jesus Christ. I stepped out in faith and prayed a prayer given through the parable of the "mustard seed." I prayed that the Lord would take the small faith that was being lifted up to Him and grow it into a mighty place of His presence where His children could come and find shelter. That was it! We simply walked away accepting that our prayer was heard.

During the next two years I continued to support the pastor by prayer and financial assistance. He came back to America one year after that prayer and brought to those who supported him an update of his ministry work. He advised us that he had agreed to purchase the property and needed financial help. By the Grace of the Lord we raised the $30,000 for the purchase of the property and enough to build a fifty by one hundred foot pole barn type structure. The following year I returned there and the church family met on the property in that new but wanting structure.

In the background is the city of Eldoret. The land in which the Lord had chosen for Pastor Watindi to build the church upon is at a higher elevation than the city it overlooks. The perpendicular building that comes out to the right was not there at the time of my second visit but was added later. The Lord fulfilled His words in Matthew 5:14 in His choice of this sight: "You are a light of the world. A city that is set on a hill cannot be hidden."

There was still much to be done to this raw church but it was a miracle that I beheld with my own eyes. The words of 1 John 1:1-2 came to life before me:

> That which was from the beginning, which we have heard, which we have seen with our eyes, which we have looked upon, and our hands have handled, concerning the Word of life—the life was manifested, and we have seen, and bear witness, and declare to you that eternal life which was with the Father and was manifested to us—

We can see that this miracle took a process through time to accomplish. It is easy to become discouraged as my pastor friend could have done. Yet, if we place our strength and hope continually in Jesus and not ourselves we will not be overcome. We may have our low points but His is the force that will lift us up out of the valley, remove the obstacles before us, the crooked places will be made straight, and the rough places smooth (Isaiah 40:3-4). Maybe there is a larger miracle developing in your life. Sometimes we see only what is before us and miss the larger picture. Jesus is always working around us and is always willing and trying to work through us. He continually waits upon us to respond with a right and proper attitude. He will do the rest. I am not saying that we just stand by and watch Him do this wondrous work—no, He expects our participation, and in the process, we will find that His Grace is sufficient to do what He has called us to do.

God uses His children as a way to voice the life of miraculous living. He delights in working through His children. As He worked through Moses, Mary, and John the Baptist, so He worked through Pastor Watindi and all who joined along the way. So He will work through you; maybe He is doing that this very moment. Isn't that a miracle—just think about it, the reality of the God of all creation being in you and using you as an instrument of His goodness and kingdom building? He wants to give you the joy of living the words that we have just heard from John, that you will see the manifestation of His presence with you in this way. You are truly blessed!

This is a good time to offer a prayer of thanksgiving. Will you pray with me?

> Most gracious and present Lord, we lift our hearts and our hands to You in adoration of the wonder of Your love for us and Your presence with us.
>
> Though we are not worthy, by Your Grace You make us worthy to reside with You and to do Your will in this place. You joyfully seek us as partners in the sharing of Your love and the building of Your kingdom in this place. For this we praise You and ask You always to give us discernment of Your will upon our hearts and minds that it might be pleasing to You. Father, we pray this in the Name above all names, in the Name of Jesus Christ, Amen.

CHAPTER SIX

The Miracle of the Impossible

With God nothing will be impossible.

Luke 1:37

How many times have we faced situations that seem impossible? For some of us, this could be a daily recurrence. It can be that way for those of us who have prayed countless times and are still waiting for the positive answer to our prayers. Yet, when we stay faithful to Christ Jesus we have hope in a living present God who confounds the world with His glory and delights in lifting up the faithful.

Pastor Simani, whom we visited in chapter one and two, is currently, as I write, visiting with my wife and me in our South Georgia home. We are hosting him for a brief visit while he attends a Christian conference. I gave him the chapters written concerning him and his wife's ministry and asked him to read it over and make sure it was accurate. When he returned it to me with approval he said with great joyful enthusiasm, "Yes! But the miracles are ongoing, they are still happening!" He is absolutely correct. The life in the kingdom with the Lord Jesus Christ is not an event but a life-journey, which is made for the faithful by the flow of His Grace (Psalm 46:4).

I agreed with him, but I asked if he would put his thoughts into words and this was his response:

> On my way to Georgia to visit my friend, Rev. Gordon, I did not share with him in advance about the plan we had on building a new church building.
>
> On the night of my arrival he took me to a cell group home church. It was there that I was called to share my testimony. What followed were prayers and a miracle of a cash blessing from the saints that meet there every Thursday. The following day when the pastor called Rev. Gordon, he revealed that the miracle was not the one hundred dollars given to us that night. Additional funds were added to it and it became one thousand dollars. This did not stop there. More miracles happened, one after the other, and by Saturday night, the miracle was at $2,950. God is just working out his ways for his ways are far better than our ways and the way we understand it.
>
> About a week before I departed Kenya for America, I received a vision to build a new church building. When I conveyed this vision to an architectural designer, he put it to paper and told me it would cost $180,000.
>
> The LORD has done this miracle and we are now at $9,550—now praise be to our LORD for all his provisions from these friends and my host. If God can provide the $9,550, he is still the same God who can provide the $170,450 difference.

I know this because it is not the first time that I have experienced God taking the impossible and changing it to the possible. Earlier in my ministry before we owned the land where our church resides, I was called to attend a short course at Dallas Theological Seminary in 2008. My classmate, who was my roommate, after hearing my testimony about our general ministry and specifically our children's school ministry, asked me if he could come to Kenya. I jumped up with joy and said, "You are welcome; my hands are open to receive you." In 2011, he called me and said three of them would be arriving. After they landed at Jomo Kenyatta International Airport, they rented a car and started driving to our town. This took them six days because they were touring and taking pictures as they drove. When they got to Eldoret, they preached in the church and they played with the children from our school on Monday and Tuesday, then they flew back on Wednesday night, and when they got home God asked them to make a calendar with the pictures they had taken in Kenya. It is through this calendar that they sold and raised $24,000, which was used to buy the land where our church resides. God has been faithful and all I can say is God is a God of miracles. Whoever believes, it will happen to him or her in Jesus Name.

After the land was bought the miracles did not end there. My host from Rockwall Dallas, Texas, by the name of Michael, asked me if he could come over and see what we were doing. It is at this time he said the Lord spoke to him to stand with us and help us put up new toilets (wash rooms). He did not stop there. The Lord spoke to him to help us have a plentiful supply of water. He further helped us build five new classrooms.

God kept bringing miracle after miracle. An Evangelist team from China with the organization called Olive Mountain came to Eldoret. They inquired from local authorities if there was any church doing community work, serving the needy children, etc., because they wanted to help such an effort. They called me and when I met with them the miracle of two flush washrooms became four. God did a miracle and the money they gave helped us put up four flush toilets. All this has built my faith in Jesus Christ and His miracles for he told Mary and Martha in the Book of John 11:25—that if you believe you will live, in Christ you will never die. I live and believe in Christ's miracles, not just daily, but with every second of my life. I believe that when He orders my steps I should really believe it and follow in those footprints.

Pastor Simani is sharing here what saints have experienced since the time of Jesus Christ walking this earth. It is what many saints experience to this day. Miracles are not just events or points of enthusiasm but are part of the fabric of His love for His children—all reflected from the Miracle of the Cross showered out in Grace. As Gabriel told Mary, "For with God nothing will be impossible" (Luke

1:37). The words, "will be" covers all further time and human events. That means that His work in our lives formats and shapes us. However, this is dependent upon our accepting His participation in our lives. God's shaping will affect both the temporal and spiritual aspects of our lives. It is all "grace for grace" (John 1:16). We often make understanding God's work so difficult, instead of releasing ourselves into the wonder of His motion as Pastor Simani has grown to understand. We often try to take control of situations and place our authority over that of Jesus Christ. Pastor Simani understands the living nature of the miraculous presence of Jesus Christ upon His kingdom of children and the joy of this reality is heard in his words.

Like Pastor Simani, once we start to accept the wonder of the hand of Jesus working in and upon our lives then our faith grows as a result, as does our awareness of the miracles around us and in the lives of others. Then we begin to see how Jesus uses others to do His work. He starts to teach us to see through His eyes—yes, another miracle in the making!

There is nothing that Jesus can't do in your life. Are you facing any struggles or situations of difficulty, maybe impossible ones? Have you placed it completely in the hands of Jesus? Recently, a Christian brother shared that it may not be that we need more faith but that we need less doubt. To not doubt is to accept the joy of Jesus's love for us. Yes, you say, that would be easy if I didn't feel so unworthy. Jesus is willing to meet you right where you are and He loves you infinitely where He finds you. He died on the cross for you—until you truly accept that miracle as your reality it will be hard to receive the full blessing of miracles that He so wants you to know. **The starting of the miraculous life is to accept the reality of Jesus's love into your heart, which is also to deny the negativity of the world—Jesus is the only source of positive power in life.**

In whatever situation He finds you He loves you too much to leave you there. He wants to lift you higher and higher into His awareness and deeper and deeper into His love—in Him it is only GOOD and it is all GOOD! He is the perfect provider and the perfect lover of our souls. He will never force us but is always waiting for us to say "Yes!" Listen to these words from Psalm 91:14-16: "Because you have set your love upon Me, therefore I will deliver you; I will set you on high, because you have known My name. You shall call upon Me, and I will answer you; I will be with you in trouble; I will deliver you and honor you. With long life I will satisfy you, and show you My salvation."

Please take a moment at this point and reflect upon your life. Where are you with Jesus? Are you willing to say, "Yes!" to His miraculous movement in your life? If you are, then you need to be ready to say, "Thank You, Lord" when He blesses you. It means taking time throughout the day to praise Him, whether for a sunrise or a kind word from another person. Think about it for a moment and what you can do to reignite your relationship with the Creator of all creation.

CHAPTER SEVEN

The Miracle of the Word

All Scripture is given by inspiration of God, and is profitable for doctrine, for reproof, for correction, for instruction in righteousness, that the man of God may be complete, thoroughly equipped for every good work.

2 Timothy 3:16-17

During my second visit to Kenya, and upon seeing that new church structure, albeit modest as it was, I could have thought this is it, God has done His work and there is no more. But He had more miracles to deliver. As it happened, I was to speak at the opening of the new building on that coming Sunday. We had been traveling each day to distant villages over rough terrain and not getting back until eight or nine in the evening. By Saturday night I was exhausted. I was hoping to get back early so I could prepare for the talk the next day. That didn't happen. When we arrived it was late and again, I was emptied of any physical or spiritual reserve.

I prayed and tried to listen to what the Holy Spirit might lay upon my heart—there was nothing. As I lay in bed in a place of open receptiveness I again perceived nothing. I decided the best thing was to get some rest and get up early to pray. I awoke around four a.m. and proceeded to pray at my bedside. Again, it felt completely dry and empty. I thought, "Lord, what is happening here; why are you leaving me stranded?" I climbed back into bed, still tired, and lay there awake for a minute, and as I laid there a bird settled on the windowsill of my room. Only a thin piece of glass separated us. It started to put forth its melody of music and I listened—it was quite wonderful. As I let those sounds settle upon my mind and inner being, a transformation took place. The melodic sound of the bird's singing became the understood word of God within my mind. I heard the music of the bird's singing yet at the same time it was completely discernable in understanding. What I heard was, "If you keep my Word you will see miracles!"

Now, there is a reason that I capitalize "Word" in this instance. It is not just enough to know the word of God and to keep it as one keeps the letter of the law, but to keep the "Word," the living reality of Jesus and to reside in that wonder, is to celebrate the true gift that Jesus wants for each of us. To celebrate the "Word" in this way is to exercise the **communional**[1] **union** with Jesus that He has given through the state of His Grace upon the believer, bringing that person into the present reality of the kingdom—NOW and Forever. Isn't this what is being said by Apostle Paul in

---

1 The word communional is derived from the word communion. In the act of communion the Lord Jesus Christ teaches us, His disciples, that He is willing to share His own being with us to sustain our existence. This teaches us that our very lives are a result of His shared existence with us and without that we would not have existence. This is true of all life. The difference with the believers is that we should understand the reality of this principle in our lives. The non-believer for the most part is unaware of the reality of this principle. As the Father, Son, and Holy Spirit live in the shared existence of each other so Jesus expects us to realize this reality in our own lives. We, as His children (John 1:11-12), exist in and through Him. The act of communion is not the act of an isolated offering but the acknowledgement of God as to the living functional relationship between God and His children. In receiving communion the believer is responding to this reality of God's offering.

Galatians 2:20: "I have been crucified with Christ, it is no longer I who live but it is Christ who lives in me"?

The next morning that was the message I brought to the church family at the dedication of that church building. The message was received with great thanksgiving and spirits were uplifted. Don't we all want to know that there is a greater good that is working in our favor in this life's journey? Well, it is true, that is the Good News of Jesus Christ. He tells us in Philippians 1:6 that he has a purpose for each of us, and that He will bring it into fullness. **However, by the nature of salvation physics, we MUST be engaged as participants in this work of Grace—there is no such thing as a sanctified bystander.** If we do that His Grace will have its full effect upon our lives.

All was well and good. It was a great celebration and I returned home to share the wonder and the joy with those who had supported this effort over the past several years—not seeing but hoping in faith, and yet now by the power of Jesus we do see! Upon my arrival home I proclaimed this message from the Lord in Sunday services—that "If you keep My Word you will see miracles!" This is the message today for each of us—to have a prosperous life we MUST keep His Word. The "Word" must be alive in us and His word of the Good News is the living inspiration of His Divine touch upon the heart of humankind.

During the next ten years the ministry in Africa continued with shifts in levels of support and those that offered the support. The economic crash of 2008 changed the landscape of spiritual offerings. There were many challenges in the country of Kenya itself. After a national election there was a violent clash between political parties, leaving many people dead. This violence was concentrated around the area of the city Eldoret where Pastor Watindi and his wife, Riisper, live. Because he had run for a political position on the losing ticket, he was targeted for death. He later shared with me that the thugs came searching for him to kill him. He was in his house and they went to the neighbor's house thinking it was his. When they discovered it was not his house they left not knowing where he lived. The neighbor didn't tell the thugs that he lived next to them. The pastor said this happened three times. This may seem unbelievable to us but God cloaked him in living Grace and made him stealth before his enemies, just as He blinded those that wanted to ravage Lot and the angels of God, or when the Pharisees wanted to stone Jesus and He walked through their midst.

This was another miracle within the larger dynamic of an overarching miracle. When God moves in miraculous ways His will realizes fulfillment. It is true that one can reject His will but the fulfillment of His will is absolute! God's plans are eternal and His work is Divine; there is no weapon created on Earth that can stand against Him or those called by Him (Isaiah 54:17). Romans 8:31 tells us, "If God is for us, who can be against us?" Do you at times feel the forces of the world coming against you? Well, if you are a believer that is a natural state. The world is out of harmony with the Grace of the kingdom of God, and therefore, its forces work against those of God. Knowing this, we need to stand in faith and rely upon Jesus and His active presence in our lives—like Daniel in the Lion's Den, we MUST focus upon Jesus to overcome the dysfunctional forces of this world. We do this through prayer and enlivened faith. This will be covered more in a later chapter.

A number of years after the construction of the first building, the city government informed Pastor Watindi that the building did not qualify as a legitimate permanent structure; it lacked structural integrity. He was given a period of time in which to build a permanent structure or lose the property. This meant that the building had to have a concrete floor, metal structure, and interior ceiling with proper electrical work. This would be a major hurdle to accomplish when you minister to a population that has over a fifty percent unemployment rate and where the normal annual income is $100.

Before these troubles arose, a mission worker from Denmark visited the pastor in Eldoret. This man was a contractor by profession and he donated enough steel I-beams to support a fifty by one hundred foot building. That happened just after the first building was constructed and before the pastor was given the notice to build a more permanent structure. Can you see that even before the pastor knew of the government's new requirement God was already working towards the final goal, and He knew what obstacles would have to be overcome and was moving to overcome them? **As Christians, by faith, we are overcomers.** We are called to be the force of Jesus and His righteousness in this place. It can be no other way! When God is on our side no one can stand against us or overcome us—we are the ones who will overcome! (Romans 8:31). In 2 Chronicles 20, we are told by God that when we face struggles we are to "Position ourselves and stand still" and it is then that we will "see the salvation of the LORD" go before us.

Is this your posture in your life as you face struggles? Are you willing to have total faith in the Lord and believe wholly upon Him? The struggles are certain. They will come against us all, but the power of God through the Lord Jesus Christ and the Holy Spirit are greater than any worldly struggle. This message is given over and over in the Bible. "He who is in you is greater than he who is in the world" (1 John 4:4).

I feel moved to pray with you right now—can we do that? Will you join me?

> Lord we come to You, wanting to believe wholly and to see the miracles that You are working in our lives, yet often we are weak— give us the blessing of Holy confidence and unmovable faith, we pray. Take what is lowly and lift it up by the wonder of Your Grace that You will be glorified. Instill in us the unshakable faith of Daniel and Apostle Paul. We want to be a part of Your living glory and to know its reality in our lives. Lord this is Your desire for us, give us what we need to accomplish it, for You are the creator of all. We thank You and praise You for this gift, Amen.

During this time, Pastor Watindi kept his vision on the "Promise of God." In Genesis 15:1, the Lord speaks to Abram in a vision and says, "Do not be afraid, Abram, I am your shield, your exceedingly great reward." This is God's Promise to you if you are willing to wholly believe. Abraham is the "Father of faith" for all who believe in the one true God. His faith was great and that is the faith we are called to seek and to possess. Why? Because the gift of the Promise is exceedingly greater than anything we can comprehend. This is told to us in Ephesians 3:20: "Now to Him who is able to do exceedingly abundantly above all that we ask or think, according to the power that works in us." There is only "ONE" overarching message in the Bible and it is the message of the Good News that Jesus Christ offers us His living presence in our lives through the process of salvation to empower us in His Love and Grace for now and all eternity. Yes, there is a requirement—that we as believers have FAITH AND THAT WE EXERCISE THAT FAITH!!! That is the total message of the Bible. Everything else falls under its domain by the power of present and living GRACE.

This is your gift from God given through Jesus Christ, by His action upon the cross and in His living Grace and the indwelling Holy Spirit. All of this is put into place to assist you in the NOW of your life and to let you live in the reality of His Promise that He, the Great "I am," is your exceedingly great gift! At this point I hope you are leaping with joy for the wonder of this gift is that exceedingly great!

Pastor Watindi struggled to complete this permanent building because he needed the funds that would make it possible. On one of his more recent visits to America, he met with a pastor who was touched by his story. That pastor took the message and his vision before his faith family and they responded with an offering that was generous enough to assure the completion of the building project—another miracle in the kingdom of amazing Grace!

This all preceded my third visit to Kenya, which took place in December of 2016. I went for the dedication of the new church building that God had promised in accepting our humble prayer twelve years earlier and that God had acknowledged in His words, "If you keep My Word you will see miracles!"

Yes, miracles abound when we walk with Jesus in a path of faith. The miracles build upon each other and the miracles culminate in greater and greater kingdom work. Consider the work of the Billy Graham Evangelistic Association and that of Samaritan's Purse—there we see through the years this principle lived out. So we see that miracles take form in different degrees of time for their completion and they are often interwoven to form a larger tapestry of His presence and glory with His beloved. **Some are fairly instant and some occur over a period of many years, but all are in the realm of kingdom-building and that is eternal in nature—by faith, you become an eternity builder!** When you do this eternal work eternity is changed forever—that is a marvelous miracle and it happens through you! **When you expect in Jesus He will give you more than you expected!**

Pastor Watindi standing with his wife, Riisper, outside the new church building, which was dedicated on December 3, 2016.

CHAPTER EIGHT

The Miracle of: "In the Name of JESUS!"

That at the name of Jesus every knee should bow, of those in heaven, and of those on earth, and of those under the earth, and that every tongue should confess that Jesus Christ is Lord, to the glory of God the Father

Philippians 2:10-11

When the Lord tells Joshua to go into the Promised Land he tells him that wherever he sets the sole of his foot he will have authority over that place. Let us hear the exact words from Joshua 1:3: "Every place that the sole of your foot will tread upon I have given you, as I said to Moses." Notice that it is said, "I have given you." This is past tense. In other words, the Grace of the Lord goes before you and has already made the way for you. You must simply walk into the acceptance of your blessing! This is the boldness that all believers are expected to exercise. There is no power on Earth or in heaven greater than the Name of Jesus, and when we walk in that power we are one with Jesus.

It was during that same visit for the dedication of the new church building in Eldoret, Kenya in December of 2016, that I experienced the power of the Name of Jesus at a new level of reality. Often times I find that Jesus calls me to His work, as I like to say, "While I am minding my own business." Meaning, it is unexpected. However, when His Spirit stirs or circumstances arise in which the Lord calls us, we must be ready. We are always with Jesus and He is always with us, but sometimes we are more attentive to His presence than other times. We must try to have the sensitivity to be open to His spiritual stirring within us. This particular day was no different. Prior to the Day of Dedication, which was being held on a Saturday, we participated in a "Woman's Conference." The conference was underway but in the afternoon, I went into town to get our tickets for the return flight to Nairobi. Afterward, I walked back to the conference, which was in full motion. It was a very pleasant day, in the mid-seventies. As I walked along the road to go back into the center and rejoin the conference, I saw a woman lying flat on the ground under the shade of a tree. I estimated that she was in her mid to late forties. There were two women standing near her. I really wanted to mind my own business but the Holy Spirit within me spoke and put it upon my heart to go and see if something was wrong with her. At first I resisted, as I was intent on getting back to the conference, but the understanding increased in strength.

So off I went towards that tree. I approached the two women and asked them if the woman lying on the ground was all right. They said, "It is her eyes. There is something wrong with her eyes." I looked down at the woman on the ground and her eyes were nothing like anything I have ever seen before. They seemed enlarged. The whites of her eyes were red and the pronounced veins were like rivers of blood. Her eyes were not fixed but darted around frantically. I asked if I could pray with her and the two women said, "Yes." I asked the woman on the ground to sit up and she did. I had a small bottle of anointing oil in my pocket, which I took out. I prayed a prayer for physical healing over her and anointed her forehead with the oil, in the Name of Jesus, and made the sign of the Cross on her forehead and proclaimed the promise of the Holy Spirit upon her. Then I asked her to lie back down and I took my fingers and softly closed her eyelids and told her to rest.

The two women and I stood there for a few minutes in silence and then with a sudden jerk she sprang up to a sitting position. She started to convulse as if she was trying to vomit. This happened rather fast. I had had an experience with an ungodly spirit many years prior to this and was aware that this could well be a similar situation. I started to pray the Name of Jesus over her and pronounced His authority, and as I did this she took her hands and covered up her ears. Now in a "politically correct" environment I might have stopped so as not to offend her, but I am under the authority of Jesus and not the world, so I continued. Besides, I sensed that it was an evil spirit within her that was controlling her arms and hands and that spirit simply didn't want the Name of Jesus to enter into her. As she had her hands over her ears she moved her head downward to distance herself from the sound. As I continued to pray over her I reached out and softly touched her back shoulder area and she violently jerked away from me. Was I to be offended and back off? No, for all believers stand in the power and reality of the Cross of Jesus and we are not to be offended by this world, otherwise we would give in to its authority and that would be ungodly and sub-human.

Seeing her body language I knew at this point that I was dealing with a serious situation and that the evil spirit within her was very powerful in its bondage of her. I intensified my position and spoke directly to the spirit. I knew it was in control of her and she was not in control of herself. Most people, who are not committed believers, are under some form of oppressive forces—yes, in bondage. And even committed and sanctifying Christians continually try to break free from various bondages. Bondage can manifest through one's own pleasure of physical self-love, under the fallen forces of the world, or directly under the force of Satan. This woman was under the direct force of Satan.

As I was in the process of taking authority over this evil spirit within her, I heard the most horrific roar come from her as if from the pit of Hell. By the present Grace of the Lord I was not startled but discerned that the force of my attack needed to be increased. Within me at that moment, as I was fully engaged in the Spirit, I focused upon the visual presence of Christ Jesus standing within me in that place of my mind's eye. I was locked in a laser type mode upon Jesus as I was ministering over this woman. It was a battle for her soul!

This combat went on for several minutes and then suddenly and violently she was thrown to the ground. As I stood over her I could see in material form her literally being "born again." Her flesh, which had its evils drained out from it, now literally started to fill with life and became animated and radiant. It was as if a wave of Grace flowed throughout her. It could be seen in the texture and hue of her skin. She opened her eyes and asked, "Where am I?"

The light had shattered the darkness and the darkness could not overcome the light (John 1:5). This was a moment of new life for her—a genesis moment. I explained to her that what had oppressed her was now gone and that she had been set free! I asked her to stand up and she did, and I enfolded her in my arms, as a father would hold his own daughter. I asked the two women standing there with me to hug her also. Those two women were angels that Jesus Christ had placed there for that time and situation. Remember, there are no random acts for Christians because we live in the realm of Grace. During the time of intense intercession I asked them to join me in the warfare and they did. Now they joined me in the time of celebration—this great homecoming.

It was a most joyful moment. I asked her how she felt and she said, "I feel wonderful!" I could tell that she was trying to process what had taken place. I again explained to her that she had been set free from the forces that were oppressing her. I told her she had been emptied and that there was now a void within her. If we did not fill that void with God's love, then the evil forces would return and return in multitudes. We began praying the Grace of Jesus over her. Again, we were using the authority that Jesus has given to His believers to be one with Him and one in Him as He is in us (John 14:20). This is a very important teaching: "At that day you will know that I am in My Father, and you in Me, and I in you." If you are a believer, "that day" is NOW! Not tomorrow or when you pass from this place into the distant eternity, it is NOW! You are living in the "present eternity" NOW! I cannot overemphasis that reality. If you don't accept that reality you will not have the authority that

JESUS wants to give you. Conversely, by accepting it, you will grow and become the light that He has set forth for you.

The words from John 1:12-13 came to fruition for this woman. Let's hear these words and see how they came to life in that moment, "But as many as received Him, to them He gave the right to become children of God, to those who believe in His name: who were born, not of blood, nor of the will of the flesh, nor of the will of man, but of God."

Having been released from the bondage of that evil spirit her first words were, "Where am I?"—She was now in a new place by the power of God and God alone. After the Spirit of God swept through her and the new life came over her she said, "I feel wonderful!" Then the words of Apostle Paul came to life from 2 Corinthians 5:17: "Therefore, if anyone is in Christ, he is a new creation; old things have passed away; behold, all things have become new." This is the miracle of the living Word! It is all within the domain of the power of the Name of Jesus Christ. In this creation nothing eternal happens outside of the power of that name. The word of God in the Bible is loaded with the power of the Holy Spirit and is enlivened with that power to be real in the lives of God's children. In that moment we could see the living reality of those words play out.

The miracle of the "reality of the Word" is that it itself is living and forming and shaping in the lives of those who receive His Spirit. A synergism forms between the living Spirit through the word in Scripture and the spirit within the recipient. They become one in the Word, which is Jesus. For a mature Christian the word of Scripture becomes more than knowledge, it is "spiritually organic" in its dynamic form. When one prays in the word of God by the power of the Spirit within, there takes place a "communional unity" with the Trinity of God. It is a state of contemplation, which brings forth a unity of presence with God when done with a wanting and earnest heart. That is what makes the Book of Psalms so powerful and real. It is the psalmist uniting his heart's longing for God in the clash with this world. It is in this way that the believer's heart joins into the heart of God. This happens by the "physics of God" and not the physics of the world—all within the dominion of the power of the Name of Jesus Christ.

The miracle didn't stop there. It would have been cruel to perform this spiritual surgery and then abandon her. It was Pastor Watindi's wife, Riisper, who had invited her to the conference and she told me that the woman came from a distant city. That is no small thing. The road system is primitive and she didn't have her own vehicle so she had to pay to ride in a taxi—these are vans that are modified to carry as many people as there is space for and the fees are relatively expensive. I also found out that she was a Muslim and a prostitute.

As the Lord's Grace is present and active with us, He had already made the way. Remember the Lord's words to Joshua: "I have given you." In other words, it is already arranged for and is done, ours is to see it by faith through the eyes of Jesus and to respond to this life giving force—that is the substance of obedience!

Riisper worked in the city where this woman was from and she said she would be willing to oversee her transition into this new life. She would connect her into one of the branch churches that was affiliated with the main church in Eldoret. See how the Lord was working His Grace upon this situation? It was not one miracle but a flow of miracles—that is the nature of the substance of the "Realm of Grace."

We met with the woman at her request and she told us that she wanted help starting a business so that she could support herself. For our part we wanted to assist her so she could break from the past financial bondage. Many of the businesses there are very basic. She would sell maize, rice and other grains alongside the road at a market place. We arranged the initial financing and her new mentor would guide her and oversee the process. Before we left Kenya we were told that one of the women in the market place had offered to share the space in her shop area with this newborn Christian, to help her get started in business. Do you see how life can be a process of not just one miracle but of "miraculous living"?

Standing with her at the church entrance after she had been freed into new life—all praise and glory to Jesus Christ!

That is why Apostle Paul, who had struggles and had suffered great pains and hardships, declared in Philippians 4:4-7:

> Rejoice in the Lord always. Again I will say rejoice! Let your gentleness be known to all men. The Lord is at hand. Be anxious for nothing, but in everything by prayer and supplication, with thanksgiving, let your requests be known to God; and the peace of God which surpasses all understanding, will guard your hearts and minds through Christ Jesus.

This is the heart and attitude of a sanctified Christian who knows the true meaning of the word "joy." It is the realized presence of Jesus within, just as I saw His presence in the depth of my being when I was in the midst of that spiritual combat. Joy is not about happiness; it is about the committed and accepted presence of Jesus Christ within us. In that way we stand upon solid ground, the rock of all ages that we will not be shaken (Act 2:25).

If you are not currently facing any struggles, you will be. It is a product of living in a fallen world that is not in harmony with the Grace of the Lord, it's Creator. We will have these struggles in various forms until we go to that final glory in the fullness of Jesus, but until then He has given us the way and the means to stand strong and be "overcomers" in ALL situations.

His known presence is the greatest reality. This is declared in many verses in the Bible. Matthew 18:20 is one example: "For where two or three are gathered together in My name, I am there in the midst of them." And John 17:26: "And I have declared to them Your name, and will declare it, that the love with which You loved Me may be in them, and I in them." It was this known presence in reality that gave me the courage to face the situation of the demon in that woman. When the Lord sends Joshua into the Promised Land he initially tells him, "be strong and of good courage." In fact, in chapter one, between the verses 1:6-9, the Lord says it to him three times. Do you think that is extra important if the Lord would emphasis something three times? The answer is yes! It is life essential! So our courage in life and in all situations should be grounded in the reality that Jesus is "literally with us"—that is His Promise to us. Remember Genesis 15:1: "I am your shield, your exceedingly great reward" and Hebrews 13:5: "I will never leave you nor forsake you."

If our courage comes from His known presence with us then where does our greatest strength come from? Our greatest power is in our loving relationship and our greatest strength comes through His Name. When the Archangel Michael is confronted by Satan he does not declare his own power as given of God but declares the power of the Name of Jesus and said, "The LORD rebuke you!" (Jude 1:9). The declaration of the Name of the LORD is made in unity with all of His power and might as He has all power in heaven and on the earth (Matthew 28:18).

Once in the earlier part of my journey with the Lord Jesus I was in a deep sleep and was violently awakened by the face of Satan immediately before my face. Everything was instant in that moment. There was no time to meditate or ponder. There was no time for alarms or contemplating my troop strength. I immediately, without hesitation, called on the Name of Jesus! I said, "Jesus! Help me!" and

He did. Satan was banished as quickly as he came. This was not a bad dream—this was the reality of the force that wants to destroy God's children and will stop at nothing to do it. Sad are those who deny this reality or make little of it; they will be like infants walking through a den of vipers. **Awareness of truth is a gift from God.** As the children of Jesus Christ we are given the miraculous power of His name! **It is our greatest strength because it is the declaration of Divine relationship!** That Name is not only the sum of all life but is the bond of the eternal covenantal love of Jesus! As His children we put on His name: ". . . to them He gave the right to become children of God, to those who believe in His name" (John 1:12).

CHAPTER NINE

The Miracle of Hope

To them God willed to make known what are the riches of the glory of this mystery among the Gentiles: which is Christ in you, the hope of glory.

Colossians 1:27

Hope is a gift of the Divine. It is implanted into the hearts of those created as His children that they might become whole in Him, complete in their true humanity and filled with joy in His presence. That is the "hope of Jesus" as He expresses in John 17:13: "But now I come to You, and these things I speak in the world, that they may have my joy fulfilled in themselves." When we unite with the Christ within us then there is joy and there is living hope.

Apostle Paul tells us in Colossians 3:11, "Christ is all and in all." There is a deposit of grace implanted into each child created by the Lord and it is a beacon, calling us home to Him. I say "home," and use that as a term for "renewed and reconciled relationship." Faith in Jesus enlivens this spark of Grace in us and offers to bring us to fullness in Him. Romans 5:1-5 tells us that we come to Him by faith; we have access to His path of life by faith; it is by faith that we stand in His Grace to face all challenges and in that "hope does not disappoint because the love of God has been poured out in our hearts by the Holy Spirit who was given to us." When hope is brought to life by faith, through the power of Grace, then the Divine reality fulfills Jesus's purpose within the faithful.

Isn't this the story of Mother Teresa? As a young teacher and nun she was returning to Calcutta on a train and it was there that Jesus spoke to her. He told her to serve the poorest of the poor in Calcutta. She was a person of faith in Jesus and had a personal and loving relationship with Him. She returned to her position at the school with this new hope within her. She met much resistance and through a lengthy period of discernment by her superiors she was finally allowed to proceed with her calling to start the "Missionaries of Charity." She expressed it this way: "It was on this day in 1946 in the train to Darjeeling that God gave me the 'call within a call' to satiate the thirst of Jesus by serving Him in the poorest of the poor."

Her hope was in the calling that Jesus placed upon her heart. Yet, this was initiated and culminated by faith. Listen to her heart in these words:

> Why must we give ourselves fully to God? If God who owes nothing to us is ready to impart to us no less than Himself, shall we answer with just a fraction of ourselves? To give ourselves fully to God is a means of receiving God Himself. I for God and God for me. I live for God and give up my own self, and in this way induce God to live for me. Therefore to possess God we must allow Him to possess our soul.

Here we see hope living in the heart of the faithful. This hope sparked to life by faith grounded in Grace gave her a new clarity of vision in the kingdom of God through a living and loving relationship with Jesus Christ. It is God who is ALWAYS the initiator within the kingdom and throughout creation, whether for salvation or for progression of growth. Notice she used the phase, "call within a call." The initial call is being in the living hope of Jesus and within that reality He forms us and shapes us, for as Paul says, "Christ is all" (Colossians 3:10). Once we realize that Christ is truly all and is worthy of all that we are then the kingdom-building can begin in a serious way—hope will not disappoint! It is only when we look to our own interest and strength that we will fall short of the glory that Jesus wants us to know.

The rest of the story, as it is said, is history. Mother Teresa went on by the Grace of God to form a worldwide ministry, the "Sisters of Charity." The ministry employed nearly four thousand people at the time of her passing. She never was given financial support by the church for her ministry but would go out with a "tin cup" onto the streets of Calcutta and receive what Jesus would give her each day—"hope realized by faith." She, a lowly nun who was a beggar, was asked to come to the United Nations to speak to the nations of the world. Many people, from the homeless to kings, would seek her wisdom and truth—all because she put her hope in Jesus.

It is "hope in Jesus" that is the turning wheel of the gristmill of the kingdom of God. It is faith that turns the wheel. Faith and hope work in unison and when placed in Jesus it cannot disappoint us—if we don't lose faith we have living hope. Seeing the witness of living hope in others that has manifested in wondrous ways should give us the direction to the right and good path of life.

Apostle Paul in the Letter to the Ephesians tells us that the ways of self-love and the world are destructive and cause a life of spiritual darkness. The Amplified Bible translates Ephesians 4:18 this way:

> Their moral understanding is darkened and their reasoning is beclouded. [They are] alienated (estranged, self-banished) from the life of God—with no share in it. [This is] because of the ignorance—the want of knowledge and perception, the willful blindness—that is deep-seated in them, due to their hardness of heart.

You might ask yourself, "How can one see the miraculous presence of Jesus with us if they are in this state?" The pure answer is that they cannot. The way to seeing through the eyes of Jesus starts by giving one's heart to Jesus so that He can soften it with His Grace and His Love. To be "beclouded" is to have a heavy fog set upon the mind—it is cloudy and one cannot see or discern clearly. Personally, I lived over forty years in this clouded state and it was when I finally gave my heart up to Jesus that my vision cleared. It was as if scales fell from my eyes. The change was immediate, yet learning to see through the eyes of Jesus is a growing process—and it is joyful in the extreme!

Let's listen to Paul's response to this fallen state from Ephesians 4:22-24 (Amplified Bible):

> Strip yourselves of your former nature—put off and discard your old unrenewed self—which characterized your previous manner of life and becomes corrupt through lusts and desires that spring from delusion; and be constantly renewed in the spirit of your mind—having a fresh mental and spiritual attitude; and put on the new nature (regenerate self) created in God's image, (Godlike) in true righteousness and holiness.

How great it is that we can "constantly be renewed in the spirit of" our minds and have a "fresh mental and spiritual attitude" that is constantly renewing! And our complete nature will be regenerated and we will realize the Christ within, and with us. As we are regenerated we will have Jesus within us and with us and that being the case, we can see, not only through His eyes, but have the awareness of His living presence with us. As King David said in Psalm 16:8-11 and repeated in Acts 2:25-26, "I foresaw the Lord always before my face, for He is at my right hand, that I may not be shaken. Therefore my heart rejoiced, and my tongue was glad." Why was His tongue glad? Because He was living in the "Miracle of JESUS" and knew the wonder of his miraculous life! When hope by faith, through Grace, is lived out then the wonder is realized!

There are many Christians who have not released themselves wholly to Jesus and are not receiving the full reward that Jesus wants for them. In Joshua 14:9 we are told, "So Moses swore on that day, saying, 'Surely the land where your foot has trodden shall be your inheritance and your children's forever, because you have wholly followed the LORD my God.'" The key word here is "wholly." Joshua was given this mission in the Promised Land because he wholly gave himself to Jesus—heart, mind, soul, and strength—which is the Great Commandment! He applied his effort wholly towards the way of Jesus in his life. It is then that his hope is realized in a real and manifested way. Yet, as shown in Genesis 15:1, the true manifested way that hope is realized for the "Chosen" of Jesus Christ is the reality that He Himself is our reward. The reality must be manifest (be made clear and real) to be a reward. That is the miracle of all miracles!

It was in October of 1962, in the wake of the Second Vatican Council decree, that a young nun named Mother Angelica was inspired by her Mother Superior to "Do whatever the Lord tells you to do" and "Do what He inspires you to do." In other words, let Jesus create your hope and by giving yourself wholly to that hope you will find fulfillment. Some years later she found her way onto a TV station in Birmingham, Alabama, doing Christian programming. She found out that the CBS affiliate there, WBMG, was going to air a series called "The Word" and Mother Angelica considered it "blasphemous to Our Lord." She met with the General Manager and asked him not to run the series. He refused to change the programming and Mother Angelica closed the conversation with this declaration: "I'll buy my own cameras and build my own studio." The General Manager said, "You can't do that." She responded, "You just watch me." The General Manager informed her that she needed his station if she wanted any airtime. He said, "You leave here, and you're off television. You need us." And she responded, "No, I don't. I only need God!" Even in the midst of this crisis Mother Angelica placed her hope in the truth and way of the Lord. Through a process of "living hope" grounded in the one ultimate truth, which is Jesus Christ, and overcoming many struggles, she was allowed to start her TV station in the basement of the monastery at Birmingham. She was given $500 in funding. Today that station is EWTN. It is the largest Christian TV network in the world to this date. If we have the faith of a mustard seed, Jesus tells us, we can move mountains. Faith is simply "hope in Jesus" and that is why it will not disappoint us. Because of her wholly committed faith in Jesus and the living hope in her heart, a miracle was brought forth.

Mother Angelica lived in the faith of Jesus and understood Him to be the essence of her living reality—that is true Christianity. She also was a woman of great wisdom and wit. She was extremely practical in her applications. I would like to share with you a few of her thoughts on faith, hope, and miracles:

> With no dedicated funds, no business plan, and no hesitation, Angelica leapt into independent television production: "Unless you are willing to do the ridiculous, God will not do the miraculous," Mother said of her sudden decision. "When you have

God, you don't have to know everything about it; you just do it."

and,

"I am convinced God is looking for dodoes. He found one: me! There are a lot of smart people out there who know it can't be done, so they don't do it. But a dodo doesn't know it can't be done. God uses dodoes: people who are willing to look ridiculous so God can do the miraculous."

and,

The enterprise was strapped for cash, more than a million dollars in debt, and facing operating expenses of $1.5 million a year. Defying reason, Mother Angelica clung to her inspiration and to her God: "He expects me to operate on a faith level, not a knowledge level," Mother said. "He expects me to operate—if I don't have the money, if I don't have the brains, if I don't have the talent—in faith. You know what faith is? Faith is one foot on the ground, one foot in the air, and a queasy feeling in the stomach."

The Father, the Son, and the Holy Spirit, they are one and cannot be separated, so Faith, Hope, and Grace also cannot be separated because they are of the same substance. They are created out (given out) of the Divine for the shared blessing of God's children. It is like a bank account that is eternally and infinitely full and given through God's invitation of love (John 3:16). Through this love He calls us to draw on that account—you can never overdraw, be delayed in receipt of funds, or see your bank closed. Once that is a certainty, more certain than your heart beat, then you are ready to activate the account as it is fully intended.

It does require knowing how to function through the procedures of the bank—Faith, Hope, and Grace. By Faith you expect the funds to be there, in Hope you spend the funds, and through Grace you participate in its actualization. Now by funds, I am not talking about dollars and cents; I am talking about the active presence of JESUS's Promise being worked out in your life—that He Himself is your gift. Let's start there with the realization of a miracle. That is the greatest and most fundamental miracle—Hope realized in the active presence of Jesus in our hearts and souls.

CHAPTER TEN

The Miracle of Manna

***I am the bread of life. He who comes
to Me shall never hunger, and he who
believes in Me shall never thirst.***

John 6:35

In the Lord's Prayer we pray, "give this day our daily bread." That can be understood in different ways under different circumstances. However, there is one understanding that can always be universal and eternal: to understand the daily bread as Grace, which is the presence of Jesus with us. In the wilderness, the Israelites received manna each day and they would go out and gather it. It would last only one day with the exception of the Sabbath. There was always a need for dependence upon the Lord on a daily basis. The manna gives reason for praise and thanksgiving, which will reinforce the relationship between the Lord and His children. When the Israelites became thirsty and complained to Moses, the Lord directed them to the Rock of Horeb and their supply of water was provided. This act towards the Israelites by Jesus was an act of pure Grace—His daily and constant presence with them. Jesus says in John 6:35, "I am the bread of life. He who comes to Me will never hunger, and he who believes in Me will never thirst." This is the one essential reality that is necessary for our survival as a people—our daily bread—the Grace of the Lord Jesus Christ.

Our daily bread shows us that He is in the mundane as well as the spectacular. Nothing in our lives is too insignificant for Him—what a miraculous reality! This day, as I write, I have experienced this truth. I live in Southern Georgia and this evening the temperature is dropping to twenty-six degrees Fahrenheit. We have families that attend our church that are very poor. Several of the families have no heat in their trailer homes. My wife and I collected some blankets we had stored in our closets and decided to take them to the families, but we didn't have enough. On my way to one of the local discount stores to see if I could find something affordable, I prayed, "Lord, You know my heart and if You desire, I will find the blankets I need at the right price, in the Name of Jesus, Father, I pray." When I got to the store their supply looked pretty picked-over. Again speaking to the Lord, I continued to look. I saw some that I couldn't afford and a few that were poor quality. Then as I started to leave I noticed two large, nice fleece-lined blankets at a very affordable price. I had already told the Lord I would be satisfied with what He would give me. Then as I looked them over a voice came on their public announcement system that said, "There is a twenty-five percent discount on select blankets." Wow, I thought, "Thank You, LORD! You are so great!" I took the blankets up to the cashier and asked if the discount applied. He scanned them and replied, "Yes." There was an affirming feeling within me as I again thanked the Lord. This type of dependence upon the Lord is essential to a meaningful relationship with Him and His empowering of us as saints. Dependence upon the LORD is not only necessary for a faith-walk but it enhances our faith and creates joy within our hearts and spirits.

Dependence upon Jesus is the fruit of humility. Humility before Jesus and dependence upon Him will open the path to being blessed. Proverbs 3:5 tells us: "Trust in the LORD with all your heart, and lean not on your own understanding; in all your ways acknowledge Him, and He shall direct your paths." In this understanding we can see that the path to being blessed is being vulnerable in Jesus. Trusting in Him with one's entire heart beckons us to a place of deep interior intimacy. It does not supplant our reality of being and loving others but enhances those relationships exponentially. Faith in Jesus is the most intimate relationship one can have and such a relationship bears great fruit. The more genuine and vulnerable one is before Jesus, the more intimate the relationship becomes. The more intimate it becomes the greater the level of faith and thus, the greater the level of blessing. The blessing is always in relational form. It may manifest in different ways, but relationship is always first and foremost with Jesus. We may find ourselves in a difficult situation and the blessing could be to have the strength to endure. One may come across hard times and struggle, but the miracle of a vibrant relationship with Jesus provides the necessary strength to see one through all of life's challenges. Isaiah tells us this: "Every valley shall be exalted and every mountain and hill brought low; the crooked places shall be made straight and the places smooth; the glory of the LORD shall be revealed" (Isaiah 40:4-5a). The richness of the words of Isaiah culminates in the last phrase, "the glory of the LORD shall be revealed." This glory is the revelation of the Lord's presence among His faithful. Here is an historical example: Richard Wurmbrand was held in captivity by the Communist government of Romania after World War II for fourteen years. During that time he was repeatedly tortured—yes, for fourteen years. For him, the miracle was that Jesus was his strength to endure and to grow in his faith. Eventually he was released, but the growth of his faith came from his awareness that Jesus was with him. The knowledge of Jesus's presence allowed him to overcome the plight of his situation. Richard had to release himself from the reliance upon his own strength into the reality of the strength of Jesus. By doing so, he gained a strength that the world could not overcome.

When we come into harmony with this principle of reliance upon the real and present strength of Jesus then we will have great peace and joy. It will give us certainty in times of trial and assurance in times of fear. Psalm 46:10 says, "Be still, and know that I am God." Therein is the substance of the blessing of Peace that Jesus offers us, "Peace I leave with you. My peace I give to you; not as the world gives do I give to you, Let not your heart be troubled, neither let it be afraid" (John 14:27).

Whether it is the simplest aspect of life or the most complicated, it is a matter of our daily need for Holy Manna—His presence. Some of our daily needs can be more profound than others. For example, George Müller lived in the nineteenth century and grew into a great man of God. He made a voyage to America and at one point during the voyage the ship encountered a very dense fog. The captain remained on the bridge for twenty-four hours hoping for the safety of the ship. There on the bridge, George Müller greeted the captain, who later recorded the following conversation:

> "Captain, I have come to tell you that I must be in Quebec on Saturday afternoon." When informed that it was impossible, he replied, "Very well. If the ship cannot take me, God will find some other way. I have never broken an engagement for fifty-seven years. Let us go down into the chartroom and pray."
>
> The captain continues the story thus: "I looked at that man of God and thought to myself, what lunatic asylum could that man have come from. I never heard such a thing as this. 'Mr. Müller,' I said, 'do you know how dense this fog is?' 'No,' he replied, 'my eye is not on the density of the fog, but on the living God, who controls every circumstance of my life.' He knelt down and prayed one of those simple prayers, and when he had finished I was going to pray; but he put his hand on my shoulder and told me not to pray. 'Firstly,' he said, 'because you do not believe God will, and secondly, I believe God has, and there is no need whatever for you to pray about it.' I looked at him, and George Müller said, 'Captain, I have known my Lord for fifty-seven years, and there has never been a single day that I have failed to get an audience with the King. Get up and open the door, and you will find that the fog has gone.' I got up and the fog was indeed gone. George Müller was in Quebec Saturday afternoon for his engagement.

Hope anchored in a relationship with Jesus is the wheel of the gristmill that produces the grain of faithful results. Miracles abound for the faithful and even the non-believers if they could only see the faithful reality. The miraculous is a sight that is beheld and understood through the vision of faith. It is that simple, "because you do not believe God will, and secondly, I believe God has!"

Simply believe upon the Name of Jesus Christ and believe in His reality, the kingdom reality. When one is "born again" as a believing and committed Christian then one MUST make a shift in reality, lest they go back to the way of the world. The wonder, the glory, and the joy is that if one allows oneself this step of faith they will have Grace rain down upon themselves beyond anything that they can imagine, from their daily bread to the most wondrous miracles.

CHAPTER ELEVEN

The Miracle of Healing

This sickness is not unto death, but for the glory of God, that the Son of God may be glorified through it.

John 11:4

My personal journey has been one of healing throughout the years and in many ways. Having suffered from a serious brain injury at the age of thirty-five, I continued for the next two years in a state that was less than fully cognitive. I had many limitations on my thought processes and relational abilities. I also suffered from serious pain in the temple area of my brain on both sides of my head. The pain was constant and quite significant.

My healing came by a Divine intervention. When I say this I totally realize it is a complete gift of Grace. I did not deserve it nor is it anything I could have earned—it was given out of the pure Love and Grace of Jesus Christ. I cannot explain why me and not others, that is not for me to ponder upon, but to humbly accept and to respond with a wholly given heart. It took me several years to come to that understanding as I initially suffered from survivor's remorse; that is, feeling regretful that I was given such special treatment while many others were not. In my mind the others were so much more worthy of such a gift. It was only when I realized that it was not about me but about Jesus, and Him completely, that I could let go of this false grief—for in Jesus all is good, lest we see only with worldly eyes. Once I came to this reality the light appeared and the darkness was shattered.

One night I was lying next to my wife in a motel room. She fell asleep next to me. Earlier that night I had purchased a book by Norman Vincent Peale, entitled, *The Positive Power of Jesus Christ*. Due to my brain injury I had trouble reading and comprehending. As I picked up the book, by the Grace of the Lord, I was able to read and comprehend the first three or four pages—that is all I read. Then what followed was quite miraculous. The reading and ability to comprehend those few pages was a miracle that brought me to a larger miracle. These few pages told of people who found their lives broken into pieces. They were shattered lives caused by their own acts of sinful choices. Then it related to how they turned to Jesus and their lives were lifted up out of destruction and the pieces where put back together. I pictured a broken lantern that has been cemented back together and the light shone through the broken pieces—fragmented light but nevertheless, light shining into the world.

That imagery of Jesus restoring these lives out of brokenness touched my heart—simply because I was that broken. I didn't really know Jesus. I knew of Him and would have said I was a Christian, but I truly wasn't. I never had a personal loving relationship with Him. Realizing the healing power that He had given to these people I knew it was what I wanted and what I needed. As I lay in that bed broken and dysfunctional I reached out to Him in a way that I never had before. I very simply lifted my thoughts to Him and in a way I can't explain, I lifted up my heart to Him as an offering—and He said, "Yes!" It was at that very moment I felt this warmth come over me and it covered my complete body. Simultaneously, I could feel union with a presence far greater than myself. It was an expansive feeling but was not an out-of-body experience by any matter of the imagination. When that feeling subsided, the piercing pain in my temples was gone and I felt a feeling of peace that I hadn't known for years—I felt human again! That was the start of my journey to restored health, which took nearly ten years to complete and in some ways, is still happening. Spiritual healing is a process even when it starts with a sudden Divine miracle.

Does Jesus still intersect with His Grace for Divine healing—Yes, absolutely! The stories of those who are healed by Jesus abound. It most often happens as a response to prayer, but sometimes He offers the healing as an outreach to bring that person back into relationship with Him. That is the greatest healing—to be restored into a living, loving, and personal relationship with Jesus Christ. That is life and life eternal.

I was assigned to serve a new church family and had only been there less than a month. After the service ended, I stood at the front door greeting people. A member of the congregation took me aside and said, "Pastor, my doctor just this week told me that I have bone cancer and have about two to three months to live." I was at that moment filled with the Holy Spirit's feeling of presence and responded by looking up into the beautiful blue of the sky over us and said, "Father do you hear what that doctor said; now Father, I ask You, what do You say?" Then I offered a prayer for her healing. She lived another five years and I was blessed to know her. She was a most beautiful saint.

This last fall, Pastor Watindi flew a non-stop flight from Qatar to Dallas, a sixteen-hour flight. He said he didn't know why, but when he got onto the plane at Qatar he fell asleep in the seat and didn't wake up until he arrived in Dallas. He slept the complete sixteen hours. He said that when he departed the plane and walked to the baggage area he became dizzy and had double vision. He collapsed on the airport floor and the next thing he remembered was waking up in the emergency room at Baylor Hospital. He said he remembered seeing all of these people working on him as he lay there.

The next day the doctor came to see him and told him that he had six blood clots, two in the legs, two in the lungs, and two in the head. His complete right side was paralyzed. He was told that he shouldn't be too hopeful; that he should expect to have some restrictions such as being wheelchair-bound. The day proceeded and he didn't get to sleep until about two in the morning, what with all the procedures and activity in the hospital. He said once he got to sleep he had a most unusual dream. In the dream he saw this man enter the room carrying what appeared to be a large electrical cord. The man walked over to the wall near his bed and plugged in the cord at one end and came over to him and placed one end of the cord on his head and one end on his feet. Then he felt this great charge go through his body. He said it was like nothing else he had ever felt. Then the man simply retrieved the cord and left the room, walking straight through the door.

That morning when the doctor came in making his rounds he asked the nurse to do the usual reflex testing of the pastor's muscles on the right side of his body. The doctor was well aware that the pastor's right side was completely paralyzed. The nurse took his right hand and asked him to squeeze her hand. He was able to grip her hand and with some strength he was able to squeeze it. Then she went to his right foot and placed her hand on the bottom of his foot and asked him to push against it, and he was able to do this with a good amount of force. The doctor was beside himself and didn't understand how the pastor could be paralyzed one day and healed the next. The pastor had been divinely healed! When the Lord wills and decides to move, nothing can stop Him for all power of heaven and on earth has been given to Him (Matt 28:18). It took several months for the pastor to regain his strength. When he returned to the doctor for his final checkup, the doctor told him, "You must serve a mighty God!"

If that wasn't enough of a miracle, there is more. He is from Kenya, a very poor country. He is a pastor to very poor people and has very little money. He was in Baylor Hospital for approximately four weeks and the bill was over $80,000. The hospital told him that it would absorb the loss and cancel the bill! Not only was he physically healed, but he was also financially healed. Healing comes in many forms. We most often think of healing in physical form but we can be emotionally healed, financially healed, relationally healed, and so forth. **These healings happen because we serve a living Lord, who is not afraid to intersect with our lives and who delights in doing so for**

our betterment and for His kingdom purposes. This is for the glory of the Father that His Son will be glorified through it! (John 11:4).

I offer you these examples as blatant evidence of the reality of healings through Divine intervention. These miracles happen in present form everyday throughout creation by the kingdom children of Jesus Christ. My hope is that these testimonies will encourage you to stay strong in the faith of the Lord. If you have not yet realized this wonder then I encourage you to open your heart to a deeper understanding of the present power of the "kingdom now." The question is not whether miracles through the power of Jesus Christ are taking place, but why are so many people not realizing them? To miss this experience of reality is to be cheated out of the fullness of the joy of life.

CHAPTER TWELVE

Miracles in the Storm

Peace I leave with you, my peace I give to you; not as the world gives do I give to you. Let not your heart be troubled, neither let it be afraid.

John 14:27

I was driving on my way to church one Sunday to lead the service. I was following a pick-up truck pulling a trailer. In an instant, the trailer went out of control and rolled over, causing the truck to lose control. Everything happened so fast it was surreal. The truck rolled over and I saw a man's body being thrown out of the driver's side window. His body was almost fluid in its form as it curved in the movement of the truck's roll. He was lifted up over the truck, and at one point, he was up in the air as if suspended. Then the truck came to a stop and he landed in the bed of the pick-up. Watching this happen instantaneously before me, I went into high alert. I prayed—it was what first came to my senses—to call out to Jesus. When we are overwhelmed we MUST go to our main strength, which is Jesus Christ! He will NEVER forsake us nor abandon us (Hebrews 13:5). He will be there to aid us (John 14:16 & Philippians 4:13& 19).

The man being thrown into the bed of his own truck was a miracle. As I saw his convoluted body forming through the air in such a fashion as to bring him safely out of harm's way, I didn't understand the big picture—I was in the "midst of the storm." Yes, he was hurt with minor bleeding, but in the scope of things he was extremely fortunate. It was a miracle that he wasn't thrown under the truck as it rolled or into the path of oncoming vehicles such as mine. Amazingly, he didn't have any broken bones and kept telling the medics, "I'm fine."

Was it my prayer that saved him? I do not know, but I do know that it could have very easily ended in extreme tragedy. My prayer was instantaneous and simply a call for help! It was urgent and not fancy or of great finesse. One of the most powerful prayers that I know how to pray is "Help me, Jesus!" or in this case, "Jesus, help them!" He is always there waiting for us to depend upon Him.

The fact that I was there for prayer and assistance was a miracle. While everyone else stood around in shock I attended to his bleeding wounds. I had the peace of Jesus upon me and I was not shaken or nervous. Jesus gave me a sense of blessed assurance as I attended to the man. But for me, the greatest miracle in that event was the fact that I turned the situation over to Jesus and placed it in His authority. By doing so, I was able to react in a meaningful and positive manner.

It is only Jesus who can bring such calm to our human nature in the midst of the storm as He did for my heart that day. He shows us this reality as recorded in Mark 4:39. The storm was raging and the disciples felt destruction was eminent. Only in their last effort did they call out to Jesus. When they did call out to Jesus He responded, "Peace, be still! And the wind ceased and there was a great clam." Jesus is the source of all miracles and miracles are often prompted by the faithful calling out to Him. Some miracles are brought forth as an unsolicited gift without the participation of the person while others are a response to pleas from the faithful; or in some cases, the unfaithful. The norm for Jesus's participation in miracles is that He will do what He will do.

As I am writing this, I just received a call from a friend who runs a printing shop. As a printer, he needs the total sight of his eyes. However, over the last few years he has battled an eye condition that has threatened the sight in his right eye. He, his wife, and a countless number of friends have prayed for his healing a number of times. Three weeks prior to his phone call today, I saw them at my son's place of business and they shared their deep concern. I looked at his wife and tears were streaming down her face—this illness was devastating for them. We prayed and placed our heartfelt thoughts at the feet of Jesus. In the call today he told me that he had surgery and amazingly, it resolved the problem—his vision was fully restored! In our conversation I exclaimed, "I just want to say one thing, 'Hallelujah—Thank You JESUS!'"

Here I am writing about miracles in the midst of the storm and my friend calls me with this good news that Jesus has answered the prayers of the believers. Do you think it is a coincidence that he called at the exact time I was working on this understanding of "miracles in the midst of the storm," or do you think Jesus wanted to make an exclamation point to this topic? Jesus is Emmanuel, "GOD with us," and the miracle is exactly that—He participates with us, He is for us, and He is willing to make the path for us—that is the movement of His Grace.

In our relationship with Jesus everything is a response to His "INITIATING GRACE THROUGH LOVE." If we respond in a living and loving faithful relationship He will accentuate the reality of His presence with us and He will open our eyes to the wonder of His miracles working around us, in us, and through us. Then our hearts and minds will grasp the understanding of "miraculous living." In the words of Apostle Paul, "let the peace of God rule in your hearts, to which also you were called in one body; and be thankful. Let the word of Christ dwell in you richly in all wisdom, teaching and admonishing one another in psalms and hymns and spiritual songs, singing with grace in your hearts to the Lord" (Col 3:15-16).

Adam and Eve caused the greatest storm in all of creation, for they disobeyed God and allowed sin to enter into their lives and the lives of all who follow. Yet in that event, God made a statement of miraculous proportions: In the midst of the storm of their lives the Lord reached down to them in reconciliation by making them a tunic "and clothed them" (Gen 3:21). He did not abandon them to the powers of the evil one nor did He discard them through condemnation, for Jesus is a God of mercy beyond all limits. In James 2:13 we are told, "Mercy triumphs over judgment."

This is the first act of forgiveness in the Holy Scripture, and coupled with this act of forgiveness is the first act of sacrifice. A life had been given, due to the compounding of their sin, which would give them a holy touch of Grace. In this act of forgiveness and the act of reaching out in reconciliation, the Lord provided for them the covenant love of Grace. This incipient seed of Grace is provided for all of His children so that they will never be completely helpless against the wiles of the evil one. He did not leave them naked, as being without His presence, or leave them vulnerable to darkness. This is a most miraculous action taken by the Heart of God, who is merciful beyond all measure. By Grace, which is the merit that they do not deserve, He affords them a path to remain in relationship with Him and goes beyond that—He puts His Grace over them to protect them in their process of returning to His righteousness. **Therefore, we can see that a miracle is an act by the God of all Grace giving heavenly favor to us who are completely lost and vulnerable without Him.** He gives His Grace in varying degrees and for different purposes, yet all is given for the building of righteous relationships.

The story of King Saul and David serves as a paradigm of the "perfect storm." King Saul pursued David. It was his intent to harm David. Saul was the reigning king of Israel and had command over all the armies. Saul had all of the worldly power and David had none, and Saul chose him for harm, but there was one exception and that was that David had the Lord on his side. The Lord Jesus Christ is a "game changer" in the dynamics of the world. The world has its power but the Lord Jesus Christ trumps the power of the world. Psalm 121 tells us that David called out to the Lord for help, "I will lift up my eyes to the hills—from whence comes my help? My help comes from the LORD, who made heaven and earth. He will not allow your foot to be moved; He who keeps you will not slumber. Behold, He who keeps Israel shall neither slumber nor sleep." And the rest is history—Saul fell from glory and David was lifted up and placed upon the throne. By faith, the words of Romans 8:31come to reality in the lives of the faithful, "If

God is for us, who can be against us?"

Grace upon Grace and miracles upon miracles; that is the joy of living a life in Jesus. It was that willful act of being dependent upon the Lord and seeking His aid that called forth the power that saved King David. It is that power that will save each of us, and I am sure that if we think about it, it is that power that has saved us more times than we can count—Grace upon Grace!

CHAPTER 13

The Miracle of God's Ever Present Invitation

For so an entrance will be supplied to you abundantly into the everlasting Kingdom of our Lord and Savior Jesus Christ.

2 Peter 1:11

Once when my son was four years old I took him on a trip with me through the mountains of Eastern New York and Connecticut to pick up some furniture. On our return trip home I was driving on an Interstate Highway descending down through a mountain ravine when I discovered that I didn't have any air pressure in my brakes. About a half a mile in front of me were concrete tollbooths. I glanced at my son sitting next to me and spoke words that I had never spoken before—"GOD help me!" I was not a Christian at the time, but the situation caused me to go to the only hope that I had. I again tried the brakes and again, there was no air pressure. Now those concrete tollbooths were about a quarter of a mile in front of us and my son had no idea of our perilous situation. Again, I called out, "GOD save my son! I beg You!" Again my foot moved to the brake pedal and at last the brakes took hold and the truck started to slow its speed. I was beyond thankful. I knew that it was a Divine intervention and in my heart I praised God during the remainder of the trip.

When we arrived home I told my wife what happened and how I felt it was God who saved us, but I didn't receive much of a response. At least there was no encouragement that God should be recognized in more parts of our lives. The next day I shared the story with my parents and again, not much of a response came forth. In a few weeks I had pretty much forgotten God's saving hand of Grace upon my life and that of my four-year-old son. Its reality had vanished and I went back to being the unthankful and unbelieving person that I was before that event. Yet, my inappropriate response does not lessen the reality that it was Jesus who was reaching out to me with His love through His prevenient Grace.

The word "prevenient" means, "to go before." When the term is used with the nature of Grace one of its meanings is that God is intersecting our lives in order to "woo" us or invite us into a relationship with Him. He is using it as an invitation to a real and loving relationship with Him through His Son, Jesus Christ. Jesus knows that we are experiential beings and that it is through our experiential portal that He can reach out to us. My initial response was to recognize God in the situation, however I let go after not receiving support from my wife or parents. I am not placing the blame upon them but simply sharing the dynamics of the situation. The responsibility in that event was totally mine. What I had witnessed was a living miracle but I didn't truly value it for the full wonder that it was. **Any prevenient form of Grace is a miracle whether or not we give it the proper authority in our lives.**

There are many times that I remember the Lord working in my life by way of this inviting Grace, yet my response was not sufficient to the offering. In every case except for one, I shortly let go of Him and returned to the world as my reality—how sad is that! **This form of Grace by Jesus is always an invitation to make a shift in our lives to a different reality—to a kingdom reality.** The first movement of Jesus in His ministry was to call His children to repentance. In Matthew 4:17, as Jesus begins His ministry He says, "Repent, for the kingdom of heaven is at hand." Immediately after this invitation He says to Simon Peter and his brother Andrew, "Follow me" (Matthew 4:19). In order to walk with Jesus, to receive the blessings that Jesus has for us, we MUST turn to Him and accept His reality—not just accept it as an understanding, but also live into its reality. Simon Peter and his brother Andrew "immediately left their nets and followed Him." They did not become other than human, but they did step into a "new" reality. There is no other way to wholly follow Jesus. The word repentance in Greek is "metanoia," which means to make a literal turn of 180 degrees from one direction to another, from focusing upon the world to focusing upon Jesus and indulging in His reality as our own.

Maybe in your life or in the life of those around you prevenient Grace can be seen. It is happening on a constant basis in creation. As with the story I shared with you, we can see that there are different degrees of response, but nevertheless, it is a miraculous event each time it takes place.

In the beginning of this book, I shared with you the story about Charles, who connected with the life-changing reality of Jesus Christ while he was in prison during a Kairos weekend. The Kairos events held at various prisons throughout the world are "prevenient grace celebrations." During the events the inmates (called residents by the outside Kairos members) are showered with the love that Jesus has for them and the reality of that present love. It is left up to them whether or not they respond—their freedom of will is sacrosanct. The responses at these events are nothing short of miraculous—forgiveness is received, broken hearts are healed, and hope enters where darkness once had dominion; in other words, new life is created.

Whether it is in a Sunday school setting with children where the seed of Jesus is being planted into their hearts and minds, or it is at a bar where a Christian witnesses to those who are broken and hurting, or at a Kairos weekend where those who have rejected life find the true meaning of life, it is all an act of Jesus calling out that there is another way, and that way is one of complete healing. That turn of "repentance" is a lifelong process of growing into the likeness of Jesus. In that way, repentance is both an immediate act and a lifelong act. As Christians, we must let go of the world and take Jesus upon our hearts and transition into His likeness. From the teachings of St. Anthony to St. John of the Cross, the message is the same—our rebirth into Jesus is both immediate and a lifelong process—yet one of great joy. In this way, all of Grace is prevenient! Jesus continually calls upon us, invites us to let go of worldly things, and come closer to Him.

"And the Word became flesh" is the greatest miracle to happen to creation in all of its existence. The "Word," who is Jesus, wants to become the reality ("flesh") of your heart. It is a moment of "Genesis" proportion. It is a beginning of a new creation being made within the creation. It is an "Invitation of Holy proportion" to God's children to find the real creation and to step out of the dying creation and into this eternally living creation. It is called the "kingdom of God" and Jesus is its LORD and KING! The "Word" becoming flesh is a Genesis invitation not only to creation as a whole, but also to each individual heart—that means to you and to me! In this way all committed Christians are "Genesis" people—forever being called forward and forever exploring the newness of an infinite God. What is your response to this miracle of Grace?

CHAPTER FOURTEEN

The Miracle of Pure Ecstatic Grace

And I have declared to them Your name, and will declare it, that the love with which You loved Me may be in them, and I in them.

John 17:23

The week before Christmas I was driving home when I received a call from my youngest grandson. He was fifteen years old at the time. He told me that his grandmother, who had just left the doctor's office, fell in the parking lot and that I needed to come there immediately. She later told me that she was looking for her keys in her pocketbook and missed her step off the curb on her way to the car. She fell flat on her face. Fortunately, my grandson took charge and got her the help she needed. When I arrived she was in the x-ray room. As she came out I could see her cuts and bloodied face. It truly broke my heart to see the one that I love hurt in this way. It was just that past November that we celebrated our fiftieth wedding anniversary.

As she went from station to station in the doctor's office, I was genuinely surprised that she was blessing people along the way. By blessing people I mean that she was telling them not to worry, everything was going to be all right, and being otherwise cheerful. My wife normally does not have a good tolerance for pain so this reaction seemed a bit out of place. I reflected on this unusual reaction for several weeks and simply understood it as the Grace of our Lord with her. It was about the third or fourth week after her fall that we were talking to a friend and she told him that she didn't feel any pain when she fell or even after the fall. That shocked me. I knew that she had shown signs of amazing strength, but she hadn't told me this aspect. She said she didn't know if it was because she was in shock, but she simply didn't feel any pain. How could this be?

I am in awe when Jesus raises His saints to a state of ecstatic awareness. It provides such supernatural comfort, protection, and strength. By supernatural, I mean that which goes beyond the power of the self or the worldly realm. We could use the term superhuman, however the most proper term might be "true humanity," for it is there where we are in a state of awareness—ecstatic awareness—of our restored relationship with Christ Jesus. It is in that state that we accept our existence in the realm of His Grace and communional existence.

This state of "Ecstatic Grace" is the highest level of relational awareness on this side of Heaven. It is biblical and has been aspired to and achieved by saints throughout our Christian history. Even though one typically achieves ecstatic grace through discipline, it must always be kept in mind that ecstatic grace is a gift of Grace granted by an infinitely generous Lord. In Paul's writing to the Colossians 3:1-4, he offers them and us a call to this higher level of consciousness:

> If then you were raised with Christ, seek those things which are above, where Christ is, sitting at the right hand of God. Set your minds on things above, not on things on the earth. For you died and your life is hidden with Christ in God. When Christ who is our life appears then you also will appear with Him in glory.

Christ is the total of our life, "who is our life." He is the sum total and to that reality, we are called to awaken—it is now and it is present. In the same letter, Paul says, "For in Him dwells all the fullness of the Godhead bodily; and you are complete in Him, who is the head of all principality and power" (2:9-10). It is in Him we find our completeness!

Let us consider Stephen. Acts 6:8 tells us that Stephen was "full of faith and power" and because of this "did great wonders and signs among the people." To be full of faith and power is to be in realized union with the Lord Jesus Christ; this is a state of sanctified obedience. If you think this is not possible on this side of Heaven I offer you the teaching of Jesus in John 17:18-19: "As You sent Me into the world, I also have sent them into the world. And for their sakes I sanctify Myself, that they also may be sanctified by the truth." In John 17:26, Jesus is even more specific about the direct practical nature of our relationship with Him, "And I have declared to them Your name, and will declare it, that the love with which you loved Me may be in them, and I in them." And the teaching in 1 John 1:4: "And these things we write to you that your joy may be full."

All of these understandings relate back to the teaching of Jesus in John 14:20, "At that day you will know that I am in My Father, and you in Me, and I in you." "That day" is the

"NOW" of knowing that we are one with God, the Father, through Jesus, by the empowering of His Grace and being in unity with the Holy Spirit. It is the NOW of the fulfillment of our baptism covenant. It is the NOW of our acceptance of the acceptance that Jesus has offered us in the power and the realm of the reality of His Holy Cross. I say, "offered us" and not given because it is for us to receive this by participation in His way, truth, and life—that is the essence of the sanctifying state. That is a lot to ponder. However, the essence is that as believers, the heavens have been opened up to us by the will of Jesus and **it is ours to "lean into" and accept the Holy blessings that Jesus has already given us by His work of Grace upon the Cross.**

Do you think that when one is in such a state that they appear magical or have stardust effervescing out from them? My wife has a very normal appearance and is unassuming. By nature she is very private about her faith and is uncomfortable when others are expressive about theirs. She is practical and has a great sense of humor and uses that humor to connect with others. So as saints, either sanctifying or sanctified, we are also humble in our true humanity.

This state of Ecstatic Grace is a gift from Jesus and is "grown into" by first accepting its possibility. The key is acceptance. Stephen, by faith, gave himself into the acceptance of this greater reality. It says in Acts 6:15, "And all who sat in the council, looking steadfastly at him, saw his face as the face of an angel." We need to be candid with ourselves if we want the most out of life, and ask why should it be obtainable for Stephen and not for us? You have the same Holy Spirit within you that Stephen had within him. In that doctor's office, where I saw my wife's face battered and bloodied, I saw through that and saw the spiritual face of an angel—and without understanding it fully, I realized she was full of Grace.

In Acts 7:55, we are told that as the religious mob rushed toward Stephen to stone him that he was in a different place than they: "But he being full of the Holy Spirit, gazed into heaven and saw the glory of God, and Jesus standing at the right hand of God." This is the miracle of Grace in one of its highest forms; the Grace of God overcomes the realm of the physical. The laws of physics in creation do not bind God—He is the creator of all laws and their relationship with each other. He sets all rules!

This is the same Grace that we are told of in Daniel as he was in the lion's den; it is the Grace that we are told of when Elijah went before the four hundred false prophets of Baal and destroyed them; it is the same Grace that overshadowed Mary and initiated her pregnancy by the power of the Holy Spirit. In John 4:24, we are told that "God is Spirit" and if we want to worship Him we must worship Him in Spirit. This again, draws us to a higher level of understanding other than our physical state. **To stay focused only upon the physical is to limit our growth in the reality of a relationship with Jesus Christ, the Holy Spirit, and ultimately the Father.**

Jesus would not call us to a place that is impossible to achieve. In Mathew 5:48 He tells us, "Therefore you shall be perfect, just as your Father in heaven is perfect." We must be open and willing to reach for this highest level of consciousness with Jesus in the "Here and Now" of our lives—it happens by faith that is fully exercised. Yet at the same time it is a gift given by Jesus and not commanded by the faithful. It comes from His generosity, compassion, and love. In our understanding of perfection we must draw a distinction between the understanding of being equal with God by the Grace of Jesus Christ and being equal to God. We will never be equal to God, but by the will and Grace of Jesus Christ, He will share His righteousness with us and it will be His gift to us that we share in His glory and be equal with Him: "But seek first the kingdom of God and His righteousness, and all these things shall be added to you" (Matthew 6:33).

The purpose of prayer, meditation, and contemplation is to achieve and grow into and maintain this unity of existence with Jesus. That unity happens by the assistance of the Holy Spirit and the power of Grace. This type of union is a miracle of great blessing, but because it is ongoing, it is more than a miracle—it forms a life of miraculous living. **Therefore, our vision becomes miraculously favored and flavored!** It often leaves the heart and human spirit etched with its magnitude of heavenly awareness. It can give the believer a buffer from the pains of the flesh and freedom to live beyond the flesh.

In the year 200 A.D., a martyr by the name of Perpetua demonstrated this reality. She was taken custody by the Romans and was tried and found guilty of being a Christian who would not bow to the emperor. She and other Christians were sentenced to death in the coliseum. As she and the other martyrs were led out into the open area of the coliseum they showed no signs of fear. This infuriated the crowd, who wanted to delight in their weakness and suffering. The animals were released and they attacked the martyrs, tearing their flesh. At one point one of them stood before the maddened crowd and proclaimed, "Well washed!" He was referring to his second baptism in unity with the blood of Jesus. He could have also meant, "Washed in the blood of Jesus!" for he had joined Jesus at that place of the Cross and it was now the strength of Jesus upon the Cross that was his strength.

They were in the ecstasy of the Spirit—in a state of "Ecstatic Grace." They were in the realm of holiness that is other than the worldly physical. The crowd rightly expected them to be in pain and suffering, yet they stood in defiance of natural laws. "Then finally they kissed each other so that they perfected their martyrdoms with the sacred kiss of peace." Simply put, **the domain of the spiritual is greater than the domain of the worldly physical. The spiritual has the power to overcome the physical in this earthly realm.**

Here's another example of Ecstatic Grace: my brother's wife, Evette, was diagnosed with bone cancer, which is known to be very painful. She suffered for some time with this condition. My brother related to me that towards the end of this illness she exhibited amazing strength. He told me of a time when he took her to the doctors. She was wheelchair-bound. The level of pain should have been extreme, but he said he watched her in that situation and to his amazement, she had supernatural strength. She was joy-filled and shared that joy with many in the waiting room. She was encouraging them, blessing them and ministering to them with the blessedness of her spirit. The light of Christ was shining through her into the darkness of that situation and she was in some form declaring, "Washed in the blood of Jesus!"

This Ecstatic Grace is the same force that is present when the saints transition from this place on Earth to the full presence of Jesus Christ. As a pastor I have ministered to hundreds of saints in that process of passing into the arms of Jesus. What I have seen and experienced is peace upon the hearts of the saints beyond all understanding (Philippians 4:7). Even those who suffer painful illnesses are given sufficient strength to endure the process. I once recovered from a serious illness and needed to visit a neurologist for a final evaluation. He asked me how was it that I could survive such an illness and I said, "Faith." He turned and looked at me and said, "In all of my years in medicine I have seen three types of people: those who have faith and are healed, those who have faith and are not healed but have the strength to endure, and those who don't have faith and how they suffer so."

Isn't it great and beyond great to know that we as believers can understand that His Grace will be sufficient for us in any circumstance? Isn't that a miracle and part and parcel of a miraculous life? As Jesus told Paul in 2 Corinthians 12:9, "My grace is sufficient for you, for My strength is made perfect in weakness." And we again are told in Philippians 4:13, "I can do all things through Christ who strengthens me." What an amazing relationship we have with the God of perfect love, if we will but have faith and "look" to Him and accept what He offers us, which is a miraculous life!

CHAPTER FIFTEEN

Living a Miraculous Life

***Now to Him who is able to do
exceedingly abundantly above all
that we ask or think, according to the
power that works in us, to Him be glory
in the church by Christ Jesus to all
generations, forever and ever. Amen.***

Ephesians 3:20-21

Dan and Linda Schall have been traveling the East Coast of America for the last fifteen years, sharing the love and reality of Jesus Christ through their Gospel Concerts. Sometimes they are at campgrounds, sometimes in churches small or large, and sometimes at RV parks, but always centered upon the gift that Jesus Christ offers His children in the "kingdom now." Dan and Linda live a life of realized grace in the wonder of the presence of Jesus. It's not that things always go right, but that they know they are never alone and that the hand of Jesus is upon their lives—actually, more than His hand, His Grace and Love. His very Holy Spirit is working within them on a constant basis as they love each other, love their friends, and minister to the general audience of God's children.

As I write this, I am looking forward to this evening when I will meet Dan at the Valdosta State Prison and escort him inside where he will put on a concert for a group of Christian residents (yes, inmates). A life with Christ is a life of being the heart, hands, and feet of Christ in this world, even if it means stepping out of one's comfort zone. A Christian who commits to a life with Jesus Christ offers the reality of Jesus in this place and gives living testimony to the words of Jesus that they "are the light of the world" (Matthew 5:16). A mature Christian takes the Grace and love that is deposited in their hearts and souls, and the truth registered in their minds and casts it into the life situations that they find themselves—always in the hope of blessing others.

Dan did not find his way on this path of miraculous living by having an ideal childhood filled with kindness and laughter. In fact, his growing years were very painful and troubled. Dan was inflicted with a severe stutter. All of us can imagine how he must have been subjected to a great many jokes and mocking as a child, but what we cannot imagine to its fullest extent is the pain that he felt in his heart. If this wasn't bad enough, his father had a critical spirit and chastised him for having such a problem. Dan grew up a very angry young man and in fact, was filled with rage that could boil over at any given moment. Then came that moment in his life when he discovered that Jesus was real and truly loved him just as he was, and this Jesus offered Dan an intimate, personal, and loving relationship. He had found the acceptance that he craved by a God who was willing to love him as he craved to be loved. This God also had the power to infuse into Dan the Grace and love of His own being and to give Dan peace inside and a hope for each tomorrow. This is something that Dan had never felt before—complete and perfect love!

Miraculously, Jesus had given Dan another gift. He gave him the gift of voice through song. This gift became his lifeline to hope and then to manifestation of joy. When Dan would sing he didn't stutter but could flow with the harmony of the music. He took what was a handicap and turned it into a blessing—undergirded by the strength of Grace. Jesus also blessed him with the love of his wife Linda, a life-companion of Jesus's love and Grace. Together they have overcome the power of this world and flourish as only Jesus can provide.

They have blessed countless numbers of people by sharing the light of Christ Jesus for others to see. The way has not been all roses. It wasn't too many years ago that Linda had to have brain surgery, in which part of her brain was removed due to seizures. Life has many twists and turns, but they found the strength of a present and engaging God through Jesus Christ. Through it all, they possessed joy and eternal certainty in Jesus Christ, which they reflected to others. This is a natural state for them. They are not acting; this is how they are. It doesn't happen by magic but by receiving and believing upon the gift of Jesus within your heart, allowing His gifted Grace to take root in your inner being and to nurture it into maturity. It is a lifelong process but one of the greatest joys.

* * *

Dan and Linda Schall

When the two of them stepped into the life and purpose that Jesus had for them they found their "Genesis moment" as described in 2 Corinthians 5:17. A new creation was formed; sadness and anger were replaced with joy and hope. Filled with the joy of Jesus's presence they are living the miracle and offering the life of miraculous living to the hearts of those that they encounter. **In essence the "life of miraculous living" is being in harmony with the engaging present Grace of Jesus Christ and joining in with the song of its existence.**

* * *

Bud and JoAnn Sawyer exude the presence of Jesus in their lives. Their positive attitude and strength in the reality of Jesus Christ is a blessing and an encouragement to all who meet them. Their gentle, kind, and encouraging love displays the real warmth of the living heart of Jesus. They are joy-filled and appropriately humble.

I met Bud while doing prison ministry. The ministry was going through some changes and struggles but he weathered the storm and never gave up. By prayer through faith and with a heart of gratitude towards his creator, he aided the prison ministry in regaining its vitality. He became a creating agent of Jesus Christ in that place. In that one instance, it served as the revival of the ministry. It was something that I watched and experienced. This is but one of a countless number of times that the Lord has actively used Bud and his wife in such a demonstrative way. Do I say this to fluff up their egos? Not at all, because both he and his wife, JoAnn, are grounded in the truth that without Jesus they can do nothing, but in Him they can do all things that He wills (John 15:5 & Philippians 4:13).

When in conversation with Bud and JoAnn, the reality of Jesus is more than a certainty: He is their Lord and friend. They share that joy and wonder as one would talk of any family member, yet this family member has the ability to bless them in ways that no one else can. With JoAnn, the reality of Jesus could not be more substantial. She listens to Him and He guides her and she knows that He has complete authority over her life. I asked her how she understood the presence of the Lord and she gave me this example. She said that she was at a restaurant that they frequent and the Lord spoke to her heart to give a word to their waitress. She didn't do this, feeling that it would be out of place. As she returned home she said that her spirit was convicted and she realized that she had not been obedient. The next time when she saw the waitress she listened carefully but was not moved to say anything. The third time they came to the restaurant her heart was again moved to speak to this woman. At an appropriate time she asked the waitress if she could share a word with her. The woman agreed and JoAnn told her, "The Lord wants me to tell you that He has not forgotten you, and He is going to bless you!" She said as she told this woman that message tears immediately started to flow down the woman's face. They were tears of eternal joy. They were words of new life being breathed into the woman by her creator to lift her up and give her hope. The Lord had used JoAnn to be the light to shatter the darkness that was trying to oppress this child of God. When one lives the life of a mature saint, like JoAnn, the relationship with Jesus becomes the center of life. Its driving and sustaining force shapes a new normalcy—really, a restored normalcy.

* * *

Bud and JoAnn Sawyer

The stories of Dan and Linda Schall and Bud and JoAnn Sawyer are examples of the reality of kingdom living. They represent the joy-filled faithful who have accepted this greater reality in a worldly place where the saints temporally dwell. The number of saints that they represent is beyond measure—creation is full of them. They have blessed us with their stories as an offering to the reality of Jesus Christ for the glory of the Father.

As Christians, we have the opportunity to walk in the present realm of the kingdom "now." In this awareness of our place in the "kingdom now," we are surrogates for Jesus and co-creators with Him. This is what Thomas Kelly, an early twentieth-century Quaker, was referring to by using the term "eternal now." We are now present in the kingdom reality with all of its benefits and power as given by Jesus Christ for the blessing of His children.

Throughout the writings of Paul, he attempts to bring us into this living reality. In 1 Corinthians 13:12, he tells us, "For now we see in a mirror, dimly, but then face to face. Now I know in part, but then I shall know just as I also am known." What he is saying is not a negative but a positive. We can see through the eyes of Jesus in this place and see the reality of the holy kingdom, though not in its fullness. This is of miraculous proportions! Remember what Paul said in Galatians 2:20: "I have been crucified with Christ; it is no longer I, who live, but Christ lives in me; and the life which I now live in the flesh I live by faith in the Son of God, who loved me and gave Himself for me." It is Christ who lives in you and me—if we open our hearts and minds and accept this miraculous truth.

In Romans 5:1-2, Paul continues to strengthen this concept: "We have peace with God through our Lord Jesus Christ, through whom also we have access by faith into this grace in which we stand, and rejoice in the glory of God." Paul declares the present substance of the kingdom by these words and he declares that substance to be Grace! We "stand" in this Grace and "rejoice in the glory of God." Paul goes further by saying not only do we stand in this Grace but we participate in this Grace and that is why "we rejoice in the glory of God." In 2 Corinthians 13:5, he gives a fitting challenge: "Examine yourselves as to whether you are in the faith. Test yourselves. Do you not know yourselves, that Jesus Christ is in you?—unless indeed you are disqualified." This expresses a renewed mindset from that of an unbeliever whose reality is in the lowly power and oppressive forces of the world. In this regard, Paul says in Ephesians 4:22-24, "That you put off, concerning your former conduct, the old man which grows corrupt according to the deceitful lusts and be renewed in the spirit of your mind, and that you put on the new man which was created according to God, in true righteousness and holiness." Paul is truly inviting us as Christians to accept and grow into the fullness of our present inheritance of the kingdom in this place. **This is not just a miracle but also a miracle that opens the door to "miraculous living," where we can expect the Divine movement of Jesus in and through our lives.**

Remember—miracles happen because the Divine is willing and able to intersect the living existence of His created children in real time by supernatural power without causing a disturbance in the natural physical laws of creation. **In a state of miraculous living this reality becomes the force of one's daily existence**. This is the reality of a miraculous life as shown by the verses quoted above and the stories shared. Jesus also commands this expectation of interaction between the Divine and saints in His words from John 15:4-5: "Abide in Me, and I in you. As the branch cannot bear fruit of itself, unless it abides in the vine, neither can you, unless you abide in Me. I am the vine, you are the branches. He who abides in Me, and I in him, bears much fruit; for without Me you can do nothing." And there are the words from John 15:16: "You did not choose Me, but I chose you and appointed you that you should go and bear fruit, and that your fruit should remain, that whatever you ask the Father in My name He may give you." These words are not about one event but an ongoing relationship that is intermixed within this spiritual unity in one's life by the Grace of the Divine—**miraculous living is about experiencing and sharing the blessings that are already deposited into our present and eternal accounts!**

In addition, Jesus tells us in John 14 that He will send a "Helper"—the Holy Spirit—to assist us in our journey of participation with Him in this life. This is the very Spirit of the living God who will come and dwell within us and teach us and guide us. This is another miracle that is offered to each of us to enhance our continual life of miraculous living. We won't have to rely just upon our own strength, for that would be sorely insufficient, but He will give us His strength. This willingness by God to be one with us in our life's journey is a miraculous reality in and of itself. It is not a miracle as an isolated event but is woven into a life of continual miraculous living.

To fully understand the dynamics of this possibility, two things must take place within us: first by faith, we must open up to the full reality of Jesus in this place and in the inner being of our hearts, souls, and minds! Second, we must be willing to think in the realm of kingdom Grace through the power of the Holy Spirit within us. When Christians are "born again," the doors to the kingdom are opened for us and we are received into the living being of Jesus Christ. Apostle Paul says in 1 Corinthians 16:9: "For a great and effective door has opened to me, and there are many adversaries." And Peter speaks of it this way in 1 Peter 2:9: "But you are a chosen generation, a royal priesthood, a holy nation, His own special people, that you may proclaim the praises of Him who called you out of darkness into His marvelous light." The word "marvelous" means to partake of the supernatural. Therefore, Peter is acknowledging that we are called to live a miraculous life and to marvel at its reality as we journey. **So Christians are required to undergo a "shift of reality" into the kingdom mindset and vision—not just a belief in His reality, but a unity with Him in this present kingdom place.**

The "many adversaries" are the powers and principalities that keep us from reaching and engaging our full potential. It comes back to the principle of "Grace freed will." We have the will to choose this life of abundance in Jesus but often we let doubt overcome us. Then there are the voices of doubt around us—even in the Christian community. There is the "giving way to fear;" doubt in the reality and promise of Jesus. Doubt is the antithesis of faith. It questions Jesus and His ability to fulfill His promise to us and through us. There are also the cultural constraints that oppress and worldly pressures that interfere in our faith-journey. All of these and more will come against us but as the Lord tells Joshua, we must "be strong and very courageous" (Joshua 1:7).

We have become "children of GOD" (John 1:12). As John 15:4-5 tells us, there is a mutual existence within us, Jesus in us, and us in Jesus. Again we call to mind the verse stated by Jesus in John 14:20: "At that day you will know that I am in My Father, and you in Me, and I in you." **Participation in the unity of Christ with us is the reality that brings forth all fruit. If this is not accepted in fullness, the benefits will not have fullness in this place. The robustness of fruit is dependent upon the degree of participation in the willful Grace of Jesus Christ.** As Jesus tells us in John 15:5, "without Me you can do nothing." The reverse is also true; in Him we can do everything. **There is a direct and proportional relationship between our acceptance of unity in His reality and the bearing of fruit.**

Isaiah gives the best literal understanding of this new realm in chapter 35. Isaiah calls it a "Highway of Holiness." Let's read Isaiah's words:

> A highway shall be there, and a road, and it shall be called the Highway of Holiness. The unclean shall not pass over it, but it shall be for others.
>
> Whoever walks the road, although a fool, shall not go astray. No lion shall be there, nor shall any ravenous beast go up on it; it shall not be found there. But the redeemed shall walk there, and the ransomed of the LORD shall return, and come to Zion with singing, with everlasting joy on their heads. They shall obtain joy and gladness, and sorrow and sighing shall flee away.

Once we as believers are brought into the kingdom, "all the rules change"—a shift is made and we are, or should be, more in the kingdom reality than in the world. As His disciples, we start to mature and learn the power of our new existence. We start to understand the realm of Grace in which we now stand. In this realm of kingdom reality we know that there will be struggles but as Jesus tells us in John 16:33, "These things I have spoken to you, that in Me you may have peace. In the world you will have tribulation; but be of good cheer, I have overcome the world." And Romans 8:31: "If God is for us, who can be against us?"

And Romans 8:28: "And we know that all things work together for good to those who love God, to those who are the called according to His purpose." This new vision clearly shows that obstacles are going to confront us, but we have unity in spirit with our Lord and Savior by active faith embedded in His Grace. This merges us into the living power of the Cross through which Jesus offers to share His victory with us.

So we can see that God the Father is willing and able to set forth this new dimension for us as His chosen. The "Highway of Holiness" metaphor purposely has physical characteristics. Godly supernatural physics—not worldly physics—forms this highway. It has a foundation, which is the truth and the righteousness of Jesus Christ—more solid than rock! It has direction and direction is necessary in order to reach the goal, Jesus says in John 14:6: "I am the way, the truth, and the life." So this road directs us towards Jesus as our present and eternal goal. As we travel this road we encounter the amazing reality that we are traveling in His time and that is Kairos time, which is God's time. It is in this element of time, His sphere of encompassing Grace, which we are brought to the fullness of His glory: "He has made everything beautiful in its time" (Ecclesiastes 3:11). The time of travel on this highway is like no other; His beloved travel in God's time not worldly time. This travel in God's realm of time is but one way we have authority over the fallen world and its oppressive forces. The highway has its boundaries, which are set by the Moral Reality (Law) of God; remember its foundation is truth and righteousness. Its space or atmosphere is one of Grace. This Grace encompasses those who travel on this Highway of Holiness.

There is even the most ancient and advanced GPS system on this highway, which is initiated by prayer and directed by the Holy Spirit, Galatians 5:25: "If we live in the Spirit, let us also walk in the Spirit." It has already been said that for the part of the faithful, prayer is an active participation in this living reality of God. Prayer happens on the highway, traveling towards the fullness of your being.

Therefore, we as believers, simultaneously live in two different realms of existence. One is the worldly existence of our physical being in a state filled with confusion and uncertainty, the other is our spiritual unity with Christ Jesus where we, filled with the knowledge and guidance of the Holy Spirit, have awareness of heavenly peace. This is the reality of the physics of Jesus for His kingdom people. **For believers, awareness is the challenge.** Awareness, guided by intentional faith, brings about focus. The question is do we dare open ourselves up to the wonder of this miraculous and present awareness?

As we mature, our way becomes known more clearly and faith itself becomes a known reality of blessed assurance. In other words, faith becomes sight—as David tells us, "I foresaw the LORD always before my face, For He is at my right hand, that I may not be shaken. Therefore my heart rejoiced, and my tongue was glad; moreover my flesh also will rest in hope" (Acts 2:25-26). **Faith is now the reality of Jesus with us, and He is also the evidence of our faith realized—the sum total; life in union with Him.** This dynamic will determine your attitude.

It is the Lord Himself who does this work (Isaiah 35:4). Then "the eyes of the blind shall be opened, and the ears of the deaf shall be unstopped. Then the lame shall leap like a deer, and the tongue of the dumb sing. For waters shall burst forth in the wilderness, and streams in the desert" (Isaiah 35:5-6). What is being described is the condition of the redeemed. In 35:10, it says that they will "come to Zion with singing, with everlasting joy on their heads. They shall obtain joy and gladness, and sorrow and sighing shall flee away." This is a state of miraculous reality!

Let us consider five necessary characteristics of the saintly nature that will enhance this vision of miraculous living:

First is humility.

The word humility is derived from the word "humus," which means the dark-colored organic part of soil consisting of decayed plant and animal matter. To be humble before Jesus Christ is to know that He is essential to our lives and wellbeing. It is to realize that without Him we do not have true life and will only wither and die in meaninglessness.

Proverbs 9:16 tells us, "The fear of the LORD is the beginning of wisdom." To have the fear of the Lord in us does not mean to be scared as much as it means to understand our essential need for Him and His life giving Grace. It means to have righteous awe, regard, and wonder in His presence—for He is Almighty. Without Him there is no life, yet in Him there is life and life abundant.

Mother Teresa celebrated her reality of knowing her "nothingness" in relation to Jesus Christ. She said, "Father, Jesus has given me a very great grace and that is: the deepest conviction of my total nothingness." And, "God uses nothingness to show His greatness." Out of the reality of humility the truth of our need for Jesus Christ is realized.

1 Peter 5:5-6 tells us, "Yes, all of you be submissive to one another, and be clothed with humility, for 'God resists the proud, But gives grace to the humble.' Therefore humble yourselves under the mighty hand of God, that He may exalt you in due time." It is the Lord who will show His glory to His faithful as He did at the request of Moses in Exodus 33:17-23. Moses, as well as Abraham and David, were humble before the Lord. Mother Teresa and countless other saints have been humbled before the Lord. **Humility is a prerequisite for a thriving relationship with the Lord, as well as for seeing and understanding His glory.**

How does one achieve humility before God? First, we do this by admitting our sinful nature and our need for His Grace upon our lives through earnest confession and prayer. Second, we bring our awareness to the Cross of Jesus and reflect its reality into our lives. Third, we examine our hearts on a daily basis and our lives in relationship to the righteousness of Jesus. We let His light shine upon our darkness. We give ourselves up more completely to His Grace so that we can continue to turn to Him and away from the way of the world. St. John of the Cross tells us that we have three enemies: our flesh, the world, and Satan. Through reflection we can give our weaknesses over to Jesus that He might fill us with His strength. Paul tells us in 2 Corinthians 12:10, "Therefore I take pleasure in infirmities, in reproaches, in needs, in persecutions, in distresses, for Christ's sake. For when I am weak, then I am strong."

Second is definition.

Knowing and living the reality of our newly created existence as children of God becomes the core of our defined existence. It will be this defined knowledge that will propel us into the purpose that Jesus has for us in this place and for all eternity. If we don't know who we are then how can we know to whom we belong? And if we know neither who we are nor to whom we belong, how can we know where we are going, or from where we came? Self-definition is essential for the fulfillment of a prosperous life.

Jesus knew fully who He was. At the age of twelve his parents came looking for Him and found Him in Jerusalem inside the temple, "sitting in the midst of the teachers, both listening to them and asking them questions" (Luke 2:46). When confronted by His mother, He responded, "Why did you seek Me? Did you not know that I must be about My Fathers' business?" Jesus knew He was the Son of the Heavenly Father and it was His sacred obligation to do the will of the Father. Jesus's realized definition of His existence was and is to this day and will be forever, grounded in this sacred relationship with the Father. Because of His self-definition, His self-awareness came alive in the will of the Father—"nevertheless not My will, but Yours, be done" (Luke 22:42). It is through this greater sense of awareness or greater connection that He was able to use His gifts and powers to free humanity—yes, you and me—from sin and destruction.

Jesus gets very specific about our realized definition in Him. As He receives His definition from the Father, so we receive our definition through Jesus—all for the Glory of the Father. It is by the Grace of Jesus empowering us that we are called into oneness with His likeness. This process of taking the likeness of Jesus upon us is called sanctification. This is a transformation of heart, mind, and spirit. It is a process of bringing His truth and love into our being. It is a process that one grows into through time. Jesus says in His prayer to His Heavenly Father in John 17:17&19, "Sanctify them by Your truth, Your word is truth. And for their sakes I sanctify Myself, that they also may be sanctified by the truth." This is the precise definition of a Christian—one that is both sanctified and being sanctified.

The Apostle Paul was keenly aware of who he was in Christ. He says in Romans 1:1: "Paul, a bondservant of Jesus Christ, called to be an apostle, separated to the gospel of God." In other words, he is under the absolute authority of Jesus and has His identity in and through Jesus. The esteem of self becomes Christ and Christ alone! He knows who he is and to whom he belongs. As Christians we must know who we are and to whom we belong. Without that certainty of definition in the "kingdom present reality," we will act out of worldly existence more than we will give obedience to the Lord. It is only by fully accepting who we are in Christ Jesus that we can fulfill our God given purpose and birthright. Paul describes the necessity of "definition" in this way:

> till we all come to the unity of the faith and of the knowledge of the Son of God, to a perfect man, to the measure of the stature of the fullness of Christ; that we should no longer be children, tossed to and fro and carried about with every wind of doctrine, by the trickery of men, in the cunning craftiness of

> deceitful plotting, but, speaking the truth in love, may grow up in all things into Him who is the head—Christ—from whom the whole body, joined and knit together by what every joint supplies, according to the effective working by which every part does its share, causes growth of the body for the edifying of itself in love (Ephesians 4:13-16).

Therefore, the definition of a sanctifying Christian is a process of growth in unity by faith, through Grace, with the Son of God, taking on the sanctified glory of His Cross. It is in this way that each of us has the potential to grow into the "likeness of Christ." Growth and maturity in this process is an absolute necessity for living a miraculous life. Paul wrote approximately sixty percent of the New Testament and, with the exception of Jesus, has spoken life into more people than any other person in all of creation. And this was all propelled by his defined reality. Jesus has called us out of darkness into certainty! That is the "light of life" that Jesus speaks of in John 8:12. That is His likeness shining in and through His beloved.

I often tell the story that as a young boy I would sometimes play on the railroad tracks, much to my mother's dismay. I would place one foot on one of the rails and try to reach with my other foot to stand on the other rail at the same time. It was an impossible task. As I attempted this impossible task, I would invariably lose my balance and fall. For a Christian there is no such thing as co-mingling with the way of the world. We must choose either to follow Christ Jesus or the world. You will fall if you attempt to do both at the same time.

Third is dependence.

In the Western world it is all too easy to rely only upon worldly forces. Currently, the most intrusive force is online technology: cell phones, apps, tablets, Google search, and more. These can be consuming and addictive if one does not have a proper perspective. These can also be used for the kingdom if one's perspective is proper: the user must remain the master and not the servant.

Many of us in the Western world want for so little and have so much that we have real difficulty seeking the Lord in our daily lives. When so many material riches surround us it is difficult to develop a true sense of dependence. What is helpful here is to realize that we need Him first and foremost for our spiritual health and wealth. The material cannot nourish the spiritual interior of our beings—that is the place where we can commune with Jesus in a state of intimacy.

Also, there are many daily needs that Jesus can provide and is willing to do so if we give Him the opportunity—"give us this day our daily bread." How many times I and others have prayed to Jesus to guide us in finding that lost article that is so very important in our lives. It could be for the lost pair of glasses or car keys. It could be a prayer for peace upon our hearts and spirits in difficult times. Jesus tells us that the world cannot give you this peace but He can and He will remove the fear that burdens you (John 14:27).

On my most recent trip to Kenya, my greatest desire was to realize more dependence upon the Lord. I knew I was becoming far too comfortable in my life and that I was not depending upon Him, as I should. I prayed and expressed this to the Lord. I do believe it delighted Him. As any parent or grandparent knows, it is a delight when your children acknowledge their need for you. So it is with the Lord: He delights in an active relationship with the faithful, His children. On that particular journey, He more than accommodated me.

A pastor friend, Rev. Bob Moon, and I set off on the trip with the intended purpose of joining the dedication celebration of the new church building at Logos Revival Ministries. Our flight went from Dulles airport in Washington, D.C. to Frankfurt, Germany. As we were about to board the flight out of Dulles for Frankfurt, the airline attendant spoke over the intercom and told us that in Germany the airlines and support staff were having strikes and many of the flights were cancelled. As we heard this we realized that it was very possible that we could get to Germany and be stranded. Rev. Moon and I both agreed that we would depend upon the Lord to make our way there, since it was for His glory that we were going there in the first place. We prayed this request and boarded the plane and flew the eight hours to Frankfurt. As soon as we got off the plane we went directly to the computerized flight scheduling board in the lobby and saw that many of the flights had indeed been cancelled. We scoured over that schedule and then came to the posting for the flight to Nairobi and it was on time! Yes, we were greatly relieved and the first thing we did was thanked and praised the Lord.

This is just one example of many events on that trip in which we could see His hand of Grace upon us. Was that a miracle? Well, I would not classify it that way, but I would credit it to "miraculous living." As a Christian believer, we received the favor of Jesus and had His Grace upon us. Remember, though we are physically on the earth, by Grace, we also travel upon the Highway of Holiness.

In 2 Corinthians 12:9-10, Paul gives a summation of the need and benefits of dependence upon the Lord in our normal Christian life-journey. In verse ten he says, "Therefore I take pleasure in infirmities, in reproaches, in needs, in persecutions, in distresses, for Christ's sake. For when I am weak, then I am strong." The statement made by Paul in verse nine is actually a response to the truth of Jesus spoken in verse ten: "My grace is sufficient for you, for My strength is made perfect in weakness." Jesus is saying that He is willing to supply all the strength that we need. **Paul gives an additional perspective that there is a direct and proportional relationship between the release by faith of one's dependence upon self and acceptance of one's dependence upon Jesus Christ** (See 2 Corinthians 9:6-8).

This being the case, as Christians, we need to understand that Jesus has already endowed us with the gift of miraculous living if we will not be the stumbling block to its acceptance. In other words, accept the acceptance! Jesus has already initiated the acceptance of our being and willfully brings us wholly into the kingdom present with the full privileges and benefits thereof.

Paul continues this understanding in Philippians 4 when he tells us to "Rejoice in the Lord always . . . The Lord is at hand. Be anxious for nothing, but in everything by prayer and supplication, with thanksgiving, let your request be made known to God; and the peace of God which surpasses all understanding will guard your hearts and minds through Christ Jesus." The rejoicing and thankfulness expresses humility, dependence, a loving relationship, and recognized receipt of granted favor. It is very important that when the Lord answers our prayers, or even when we don't pray but we can see His Grace bless us or someone else, that we give thanks and praise. In human relationships it is considered rude to not thank someone for being kind or polite to us. The Lord is not different—thanksgiving and praise is a post stamp on the expression of love extended to Him. **The cultivated sense of dependence upon the Lord will draw you closer to the Lord and magnify the realized wonder of His presence with you.**

Fourth is passion.

As we have heard, Paul tells us in Galatians 2:20, it is Christ who lives in us. By that very nature we are instilled with the passion of Jesus. We have also heard in Romans 5:5 that the "love of God has been poured out in our hearts by the Holy Spirit who was given to us." Passion comes from a vibrant and living connection of the human spirit with the Spirit of God. The passion of God comes to us as a gift of Divine Grace; yes, a miraculous act calling forth a miraculous response. Yet, even if it is a Divine gift and instilled within us, we must be awakened to its reality to respond appropriately.

When the believer releases himself or herself to the joy within, passion is at its full potential—again, to accept the acceptance that Jesus has already offered us and through which He has already made the way for us. As we have just learned, if we depend upon Jesus more in our lives, that awareness of joy within will expand. **Our faith-passion is a factor in the extent to which we realize the wonder of His greatness at work for us and within us.**

Once awakened to the reality of this Divine unity within us, we experience a powerful feeling of inward expansiveness. This inward expansiveness is the result of our hearts being in unity with the heart of Jesus. Then we, like Jesus, want to share that Divine Love and reality with others. Passion is a response to the initiating and present Grace of Jesus Christ.

Jesus tells us that this desire to share His truth with others is what He expects from us. Matthew 5:16 says, "Let your light so shine before men, that they may see your good works and glorify your Father in heaven." Passion emits the light that shines from the wonder within you. This wonder within reflects off of the Passion of the Cross of Jesus—it is a direct radiance into our hearts and souls as His believers.

Fifth is intentionality.

Once grounded in humility, defined, passionate, and dependant upon the Lord, there is still the necessity of intentionality. If humility is the path and definition is the vehicle, then dependence becomes the fuel and passion is the spark that ignites the fuel. To this point, all of this is "potential," yet, potential becomes nothing without a guiding force or governing presence. Therefore, intentionality is the driver with his/her hands upon the steering wheel and foot hovering over the accelerator and brake. You become the force of intentionality to bring the Lord's presence to meaning in this place. The Lord provides the vision, the Holy Spirit offers the guidance, but only intentionality sets the motion. **No one will advance in life without being intentional; it is what moves us from position A to position B.** Position "A" is the place of being tossed here and there by the waves of the world. Position "B" is being on the "Highway of Holiness." What we experience on the Highway of Holiness is living the miraculous life—filled with Grace and Truth.

To help you bring about a greater awareness of your miraculous potential on this journey of life I want to encourage you to be intentional in certain areas. One such area is journaling. This is different than an effort directed solely towards introspection. This effort will help you see and record the light of the Lord with you and about you. As you go from day to day, I want to encourage you to record what the Lord speaks to you through Scripture, through the given word of the Holy Spirit upon your heart, and/or spoken to you through fellow believers or circumstances. This doesn't have to be done on a timetable but it should be an intentional discipline.

You may want to record how you have seen the hand of the Lord move in your life or in the lives of others. There may be one particular occasion when you felt really close to the Lord—journal it! It can be a great resource for you to use in the future, for writings, or talks. It can also become a great treasure for you over a period of time.

You may want to just sit down and have a conversation with the Lord or express your feelings about the condition of your current relationship. This can also help you work through the struggles that you are encountering. As you ponder the particular situation, think if there is a Scripture story or verse that applies—you are helping yourself see through the enlivened reality of the word of God. Remember the word of God is "power loaded with the Holy Spirit."

Journaling is also a great way to sing praises to the Lord—isn't this what we see in the Book of Psalms? Our true life is all about intersecting with the Lord in a living, loving, and vibrant relationship that cascades out to others. As you journal you will see new facets open up, which will allow you to more fully explore your relationship with the Lord.

To enhance your perspective of miraculous living, I would also encourage you to commit to daily reflection. This can be incorporated into the journaling process but it has a different purpose. The purpose of reflection is to bring to mind your recent actions in relation to the Lord—your thoughts and behavior during a given time period. You may want to ask yourself, did I show the likeness of Christ in my travels today? Was there something that you could have done differently that would have pleased Jesus? You might want to ask yourself, where and why am I struggling in my relationship with Jesus? What Bible teachings or verses can help me in this area? Maybe I need to discuss this with a mentor or pastor—the Lord will place people in your path to aid you. Through prayer seek discernment in obtaining guidance.

Henri Nouwen, a great Christian writer of the Roman Catholic family, said of our relationship with the Lord: "To pray . . . means to think and live in the presence of God." This means that we are not only in constant contact with the Lord but that we can have the sense of certainty of His presence with us at all times. This should be a proper state of mind for all Christians. If we are constantly aware of our presence with Christ then we can do as the Apostle Paul bids us: pray without ceasing (1 Thessalonians 5:17). Use the Humility-Definition-Dependence-Passion-Intentionality checklist to help calibrate your daily walk with the Lord. First, it will help you remain grounded. Secondly, it will give you clarity as to where you need to place your spiritual efforts for growth and balance in your faith-journey.

By doing this, it allows each of us to be in a constant state of reflection with the Lord, which will give us greater understanding of the preciousness of His miraculous presence with us. Then the awareness that Jesus so wants you to know will become clearer and clearer to you—until you will discover what Jesus has always wanted you to know: "YOU ARE A LIVING MIRACLE!" Created in Jesus, as we are told by the Apostle Paul in Galatians 2:20, "it is no longer I who live, but Christ who lives in me," we live in unity with Christ Jesus, in His being (Acts 17:28). Thus, we see through His eyes. Kairos is the understanding that we have a present and realized existence in the living Grace of Jesus Christ. His Grace allows His faithful saints to unite in His time and space. In this Kairos existence, time has a different reference and nature. The relativity of time becomes a function of faith and Grace. We are no longer removed from Christ but united into His reality, into His sphere of existence. We are one with the saints, past and present, and in continuity with their faith and likeness. This is miraculous living in the highest order—a form of "Ecstatic Grace."

As the Lord would have it, I was reminded of this during a recent Kairos weekend in prison ministry. It was our fourth day in the four-day intensive session with forty-five residents (inmates). We were in the conference room and there was a great deal of activity. It was during a time of recess. People were talking and moving about and as I glanced across the room, unsuspecting, my eyes settled upon Gerald, a fellow Kairos minister. As I looked at him, something amazing but understandable happened: I saw him through the eyes of Jesus.

His face appeared beatified. It was not that it no longer appeared human, but in fact, appeared "truly human." I was looking from a distance of approximately forty feet, and this was not just a second's glance but a concentrated period of time for discernment. What I saw was a face with a tender glow that appeared to have a radiance that animated life at a higher realm of being. I can give it no other term than to say that it was "angelic" in nature.

It was at that moment that I knew I had seen the face of Stephen as spoken about in Acts 6:15. This is what the Lord allowed me to see by His gift of Grace—that the faithful live in this realm of reality. This man that I saw in such a form is an apostle for Christ. Yet, he was not always so animated in Christ. It was only after the Lord brought him back from death that his heart erupted into gladness for the wonder of the Lord. A tree fell upon him and he was pinned beneath this twenty-four-inch diameter weight. As he tells it his chin was forced flat against his kneecaps. In his words, he was shaped like a closed billfold wallet.

His son was a doctor and was present as they were trying to take down some trees when this particular tree came crashing in a direction that they didn't expect and landed on Gerald. He was pinned and could not move; in fact, he showed no signs of life. His son immediately ran to him and checked his vital signs and pronounced him dead. However, God had another plan. After the many hours of attempting to free him and the medics working on him, he finally showed signs of life. He was flown to a regional hospital that could handle trauma cases. God brought him back to life and in fact, when the trauma doctor called his son he was told that Gerald didn't have any of the internal damage that would have been expected in a case such as his. Gerald was blessed to have new life and a new opportunity to live for the right reasons. This experience instilled Gerald, and I would think his wife and son as well, with boldness in his heart and pure thankfulness! Gerald said that the greatest change for him has been to realize that it is all about relationships. That is the essence of life and that is the message he shares.

So in his life we see multi-miracles culminating into the robust wonder of living Grace, as Christ is the one who now lives in him. No power on Earth could accomplish this and set him apart in such a way as to proclaim the present glory of Jesus Christ. This is truly a miraculous flow of life culminating in a living chorus of thanksgiving!

CHAPTER SIXTEEN

The Miracle of Giving Thanks!

Enter into His gates with thanksgiving, and into His courts with praise. Be thankful to Him, and bless His name.

Psalm 100:4

The other day, my wife and I delivered some food to a needy family. There were many children there as two families live in one singlewide trailer. When we gave out the food everyone was caught up in the excitement of the gift and took what was given and ran into the house. I stood there at the back of our car for a moment, catching my breath, and one of the younger girls returned and came up to me and stood there and said in a soft voice, "Thank you for giving us the food." My un-thought-through genuine response was, "Thank you, for your thank you!" It was a sweet moment.

In Luke 17, Jesus tells us that there were ten lepers that He had cleansed and then He sent them to show themselves to the priests as was required by their religious law. We are told that "one of them, when he saw that he was healed, returned, and with a loud voice, glorified God, and fell down on his face at His feet, giving Him thanks." Then Jesus said, "Were there not ten cleansed? But where are the nine?" One would have to pity the nine who did not realize where their blessings truly came from and from where all blessings come. It also shows that the nine didn't grasp the reality of a living and present relationship with Jesus—they simply didn't get it.

In personal relationships, showing respect, regard, and appreciation for the love that extends from another is essential to that relationship; but not just to the relationship—it is essential to the welfare of our own hearts and spirits. Giving thanks is acknowledging and appreciating the other and reminding our conscious self that we are in fact dependent upon Jesus. The act of directing focus away from oneself aids in the reality of proper humility. That is to say, without the other—Jesus, in this case—we would be nothing and have nothing—but in Him we have everything. This is why Paul tells us in Philippians 4:6, "Be anxious for nothing, but in everything by prayer and supplication, **with thanksgiving,** let your requests be made known to God; and the peace of God, which surpasses all understanding will guard your hearts and minds through Christ Jesus." The linchpin of this statement by Paul is "with thanksgiving." It is the thankful spirit of the heart that animates the request before God the Father and bonds the element of relationship.

I have mentioned the importance of this understanding throughout this book, but now I bring it to full emphasis. We must ask ourselves, you and me: do we thank Jesus enough for what He has done for us? How many times a day do we stop and give Him praise or thanksgiving? It could simply be thanksgiving for keeping us safe through the night or thanks for the peace He gives us in stressful moments. Remember,

King David praised the Lord seven times a day—that is an intimate, loving, and affectionate response to a true reality! (Psalm 119:164). I encourage you to take moments during the day to silently or verbally thank Jesus, and I do believe with all my heart that He will say to you, "Thank you for your thank you!"

CHAPTER SEVENTEEN

Miracles Abound!

And there are also many other things that Jesus did, which if they were written one by one, I suppose that even the world itself could not contain the books that would be written. Amen.

John 21:25

A newborn baby held in the arms of the mother, surrounded by the love of the father and relatives—that is not only a miracle realized but a miraculous movement within life—if it is realized for what it is—the living hope and joy that only a present and engaging God could create in the human heart. New life is the miracle of God through Jesus Christ—in birth and in hope. Each new life brings hope for the future of each family and for humanity as a whole.

The parent or grandparent who speaks words of life into their children is a miracle to that young child. The pastor who proclaims the Good News of Jesus Christ and gives hope to the seeking, the hurting, and lost is a miracle in the forming of a better creation. The elected officials and administrators who function daily with a "spirit of excellence" that was witnessed in Daniel, are all miracles to the people they serve.

Through the touch of a nurse's gentle hand healing is felt. Through the years of study and experience the doctor's sense of care and skills help lead God's children to safety and health. The medicine that the doctor prescribes comes to your aid and gives you comfort. The hands, eyes, and heart of the surgeon are there to restore you to health and wellbeing. The marvels of the technology from x-rays to MRIs and beyond are all signs of the blessings of God being poured out upon His children—all miracles. **For it is God the Father, in and through Jesus Christ, above all, that wants us to live a miraculous life—"On earth as is in heaven"** (Matthew 6:10).

The first responders and military are there every day to protect us and come to our aid in times of crisis. The teachers who pour themselves out for us are there so that we have the opportunity to advance in a good and learned path of life. Whether or not they are believers is not the issue; God will use them for His Grace outpouring—"And of His fullness we have all received, and grace for grace" (John 1:16). If they happen to be believers then the blessing will hopefully be recognized for what it is, the Grace outpouring of Jesus Christ upon His children. Once recognized for what it is then adoration should be the natural response. The kingdom present becomes realized for its present reality and encompassing Grace and Love.

When a broken heart heals, when a lonely and anxious soul gladdens, when a mind receives a spirit of peace, and the perfect Love of Jesus overcomes fear, then a miracle has been experienced. When a woman or a man imprisoned attends a Kairos weekend and finds that Jesus Christ is real and that they can receive forgiveness and can have eternal life that is a miracle. When someone attends a church service and a song or message touches their heart and brings them closer to an understanding of a real relationship with Jesus Christ, a miracle has occurred.

The list is almost endless and it abounds beyond measure. From the blessing of our daily bread to the raining of the Grace upon our lives, each day we are not only living the miraculous life but we are also the miracle—filled with His love, empowered by the Holy Spirit within, strengthened by His Grace, anchored upon the rock of His foundation in this place while at the same time, spiritually united in the sphere of Heaven where no force on Earth is able to prosper against us—wouldn't you say that that is miraculous? You are a living miracle! Even greater than that, you are a miracle that creates other miracles by sharing and encouraging each other in this most Grace-filled life all in a Genesis process—being co-creators with Jesus Christ. In this I bid you to grow into your blessings—they have already been prepared for you!

> *"Did I not say to you that if you would believe you would see the glory of God?"*
>
> John 11:40

Bibliography

Arroyo, Raymond. Mother Angelica: *The Remarkable Story of a Nun, Her Nerve, and a Network of Miracles.* New York: Doubleday, 2005.

Beasley-Topliffe, Kieth, ed. *The Sanctuary of the Soul.* Nashville: Upper Room Books, 1997.

Greer, Wendy Wilson, ed. *Henri J. M. Nouwen: The Only Necessary Thing.* New York: Crossroad, 1999.

Job, Rueben P., and Shawchuck, Norman. *A Guide to Prayer for Ministers and Other Servants.* Nashville: Upper Room, 1983.

Kolodiejchuk, Brian, ed. *Mother Teresa: Come Be My Light.* New York: Doubleday, 2007.

St. John of the Cross. *The Dark Night of the Soul.* New York: Doubleday, 1990.

Wilson-Kastner, Patricia, et al. *A Lost Tradition: Women of the Early Church.* Washington University Press of America, 1981.

Continue to learn and grow in the living wonder of Jesus at lifeadvancenetwork.com.

Join the Miracle:

Here you can continue to learn more about the nature of miracles. You can hear the stories of others who see the miracles of Jesus in their lives. There will be an open forum for dialogue where you will have the opportunity to share your own stories.

Share the Miracle:

As you have read in this book, there are many Christians offering the love of Jesus to others. Lifeadvancenetwork.com will offer you an opportunity to participate in ministries grounded in Jesus. You will be able to see the effects of your participation and see miracles in the making.

Be a Miracle:

Ultimately, it is all about being the living miracle to creation that the Lord Jesus has created you to be. In this forum you will be encouraged and directed in your growth to share the living light of Jesus.

Lifeadvancenetwork.com:

Once you go to the website, you can enjoy the general offering or connect directly to the Miracles Abound Page, which is at the top of the Home Page. There are two blogs, one general and one under the banner of Miracles Abound.

It is my hope that this community of dialogue will open up "a great and effective door" for you (1 Corinthians 16:9).

It is through this portal that He will "do exceedingly abundantly above all that we ask or think, according to the power that works in us (Ephesians 3:20).

www.ingramcontent.com/pod-product-compliance
Lightning Source LLC
Chambersburg PA
CBHW052036070526
44584CB00016B/2062